DISCARDED

THE SEETHING AFRICAN POT

THE SEETHING AFRICAN POT
A Study of Black Nationalism
1882–1935

by
DANIEL THWAITE

NEGRO UNIVERSITIES PRESS
WESTPORT, CONNECTICUT

Originally published in 1936 by
Constable & Co., Ltd., London

Reprinted 1970 by
Negro Universities Press
A Division of Greenwood Press, Inc.
Westport, Connecticut

SBN 8371-3757-8

Printed in United States of America

CONTENTS

		PAGE
I	THE BIRTH OF ETHIOPIANISM IN SOUTH AFRICA	1
II	THE GROWTH OF ETHIOPIANISM IN AFRICA	31
III	SECRET SOCIETIES OF CENTRAL AFRICA	70
IV	BLACK NATIONALISM FALLS INTO THE RUSSO-GERMAN TRAP	144
V	ETHIOPIA A PAWN IN THE GAME	189
APPENDIX I.	CHURCH ACTIVITIES IN NUMBERS	236
APPENDIX II.	THE WAHALE REBELLION	237
APPENDIX III.	NATIVE SEPARATIST CHURCHES	240

I THE BIRTH OF ETHIOPIANISM IN SOUTH AFRICA

Africa is today in the throes of a crisis caused by the violent anti-white movement which has been fermenting in Central and South Africa during the last 50 years. This movement, the product of a carefully tended black nationalism and racial self-consciousness among the Bantu tribes, now asserts a right to self government and independence. This advanced claim is put forward irrespective of the mental and moral aptitude of its supporters or of their business capacity, as is shown, not only by their inability to conduct their own affairs but also by their failure to perceive the chaos to which they would revert if the white man's restraining hand were removed and their own leaders resumed unhampered their former abuse of power.

It must be admitted that the native has a very strong case and that his unpleasing transmutation must be laid wholly at the door of the white man, since, in many instances, the white man has deliberately sought to transform the native that he might exploit him for his own ends. In others, where his motives were charitable and his end philanthropic he strove, with an equally ruthless and ignorant disregard of the customs and traditions of the peoples among whom he was working, to impose his outlook upon them.

In the early days of white penetration many white men landed in Africa with preconceived notions of what they would find there and how they would deal with the situation. Some mistakenly regarded the native as a clean slate on which they could write anything they chose, and expected their injunctions to remain sacred and unchallenged however alien to native established rule. In Biblical parlance, they thought that all they had to do was to pipe the tune and the natives would be honoured to dance to it. They never imagined that they might choose altogether a different one for themselves and elect to dance to that, once the beauty of the old tune was destroyed for them. Others based their dealings on the conviction that anything the black man did or thought was vile. They set out to uproot him body and soul from his surroundings, dumping him down in a class by himself with all his old traditions shattered and his beliefs trampled upon: they expected him to accept and live up to ideals that were antagonistic to his feelings, that outraged all that had been sacred to him until yesterday and cut him off from his family and tribe, expecting him to blossom in a day from a raw savage into a black model citizen on a reduced scale of western civilization and white perfection. In some ways it was not so much the fault of the individuals themselves as of the general attitude of the times. It was deemed unnecessary for white men to have any special training before dealing with and being put in charge of natives. It was a common assumption that work in the colonies required men of less education than work at home, so the colonies became a sort of clearing-house for failures and worse. This unfortunately applied equally to the missionary as to other callings, and until quite recently it was the prevalent opinion that the Gospel could be better preached and interpreted to ignorant and degraded savages by less intellectual and less educated men. Of course, in this case the whole line of reasoning was wrong, for the natives were not as savage and degraded as was supposed, and anyway the more difficult they were to deal with, the better equipped their teachers should have been.

Anthropology, ethnology and psychology were then still in their infancy, preserved in jealously-guarded incubators in the forcing-houses of the universities for the exclusive use of ponderous scientists. That they should form part of the equipment of civil servants and missionaries was not discovered to be essential until within the last few years. Nor has the necessity yet been realized to the extent it deserves, that such people should at the very least thoroughly understand, if not correctly speak, the language of the tribes under their care. Missionaries and magistrates can still be found transacting all their business through the medium of an interpreter, one as likely as not belonging to another tribe, who is not familiar with the intricacies of the language he is supposed to translate, or with the customs of the people whose interests he should explain. He is liable therefore to make the grossest mistakes even when he is honestly doing his best; and that he is always honest can by no means be taken for granted, as frequently an interpreter will accept a bribe not only from one, but from both parties in court, in which case he will merely tell the magistrate what he considers most likely to favour the client of his choice, and will translate into the vernacular only what he considers good for his audience to hear.

Direct contact with the natives and direct communication with them, is not considered an integral part of the duty of white officials, and the misunderstandings that arise, though they sometimes make good and amusing stories, lead too often to tragic and grave miscarriage of justice.

Only recently has the white man begun to realize his error in not studying native religions, customs and languages before attempting to modify native life and influence native conduct. Of late a better understanding of primitive life has been attained thanks to the careful investigations of independent travellers and of more efficiently equipped civil servants and missionaries.

Much study is now being given to native languages which are revealing a wholly unsuspected and astonishing variety, an accuracy in the use of extensive vocabularies and nice distinctions in spiritual concepts. In their former ignorance of the African languages missionaries and travellers created the legend that they were poor, uncouth and inexact, deducing this etymological poverty from the native's inability to translate words which conveyed no meaning to him; terms relating to articles, clothing perhaps, or instruments of which the native had had no experience, and to abstract subjects which were foreign to him. For example, the fact that most Bantu languages cannot describe the various shades of colours, led to the erroneous impression that the Africans were colour-blind, whereas they devote most meticulous care to matching their beads or other material for their adornments and sartorial effects. Moreover rarely did they allow for the innate secretiveness of the natives which prompts them to conceal as long as possible from strangers any information concerning themselves. Some African tribes are even today alleged to have no word for "truth" in their language and are believed therefore to have no idea of its meaning. Tomorrow some investigator may discover such a word to be synonymous with foolishness, or childishness, or some other form of mental weakness; for the natives are not ignorant of the meaning of truth, but they are trained from childhood to mask it, conceal and disguise it in the interests of their personal and tribal safety.

In the early days however the white man judged the black by the light of his own ignorance, indulgently or severely according to the grace that warmed his heart; he built up a report, both official and private, so unintentionally misleading and so wide of the mark as to bring about a complete misconception of Bantu life and thought that was to have very far-reaching consequences. He made it his errand—and boasted of his achievement—to raise the natives at one bound from utter savagery to a mockery of white civilization, instead of striving to set their feet on the path of rational development, allowing them meanwhile to retain as many of their old inherited customs as make for social order and standards. He never reflected that education ought to take into account the life not only of the individuals but also of the community to which they belong and the whole environment which presses upon them; that it is unwise to break down the wholesome restraints of tribal discipline on the plea that they are based on superstition and the abuse of power, until the pupils have learnt to adapt themselves and to accept new lines of thought and behaviour. Whether the innovations were desirable

THE BIRTH OF ETHIOPIANISM IN SOUTH AFRICA

or not, and whether the Bantu tribes would have benefited or not by an attempt to adopt the white man's social organization and moral code, it remains an indisputable fact that generations of slow evolution are required to dislodge and modify beliefs and institutions which are the outcome of material and spiritual surroundings and conditions, which must in themselves be changed before another set of beliefs and institutions can be assimilated.

No effort was made to examine the existing order before overthrowing it. Not finding in Africa any trace of the paraphernalia of justice he had been accustomed to revere in his own country, the white man, blinded by his overweening sense of superiority that bade him judge everything he saw offhand before investigating it, perceived nothing more, in the chief squatting with his court in the shade of a tree, than a ludicrous embodiment of apocryphal law and a semblance of order. That the fundamental principles of justice, unadorned by any panoply or frippery, though substantially different in the African conception from the European interpretation of its ends, could be eminently sound never occurred to him at all.

In Africa punishment, in its terribly retributory philosophy, includes three basic concepts of indisputable logic, for it has a threefold object. Punishment to the offender, indemnity to the injured and contribution to the chief for having learnt the law of the tribe and troubled on that occasion to mete it out. It is a sequence from which there is no escape except by the power of witchcraft; only charms of sufficient potency to protect from detection or confuse the judges at the trial could save the culprit from the consequences of his act. This is no place to investigate the part of witchcraft as relating to criminals, though it is a subject that will crop up again later. All that can be said now is, that when charms were insufficient to prevent detection by smelling out, or the charge was substantiated by witnesses, trial followed with a swiftness undreamt of in white countries.

Trials rarely lasted more than a day or two, and sentence was pronounced verbally and on the spot without the aid of scribes or ushers. Physical punishment ran the whole gamut from chopping off a finger to capital punishment, but as a rule it was indulged in only by some occasional and bloodthirsty tyrant, for even primitive society was well awake to the greater contribution that is made to the safety and strength of the tribe by a live and hearty member as compared with a dead or maimed one. Anyway, it did not preclude fines, for indeed it generally automatically included forfeiture to the chief of all the accused's possessions down to his women and children. Torture for the mere pleasure of inflicting bodily pain also was

THE BIRTH OF ETHIOPIANISM IN SOUTH AFRICA

less frequent than one is generally inclined to suppose, and many students of primitive life are inclined to affirm that when it was done, like many of the practices of secret societies, it was more as a form of entertainment for the chief and tribe than with the intention of inflicting pain as punishment for the crime or as solace to the feelings of the injured party. In short it was an African rendering of the arena of more progressive countries.

Punishment in a primitive community is retribution for an act of hostility to somebody or something, or for the unobservance of a religious duty or taboo, or law of the country. The act may be secret, revealed only by "smelling out," or overt, such as murder, rape, theft, stock-stealing, etc. The injured party or his family have the right to an indemnity, and when the culprit does not, or cannot pay it, his family are answerable for it. Thus all members of a family are responsible for the good behaviour of each other, and each village for that of all its members. Money, before the advent of the white man, was unknown, the only form of exchange being in animals. In some tribes only cattle counted for exchange; in others there was a sort of tariff of equivalents, so many sheep or goats for each head of cattle. In the same way there was a tariff of fines: murder, so many head of cattle; rape, in itself so many, and so many more when it was followed by the birth of a child, etc. A man could be rich one day, and the next, by some rash act of lust or anger, be completely impoverished. Unsatisfied with so simple an organization, the white man transplanted into Africa his own theories of punishment. He abolished the indemnity for wrongs to widowed wife and orphaned children or outraged girl. He no longer insisted that stolen cattle should be returned over and above the fine paid for the robbery. By his law a criminal is taken to a hut larger and more comfortable than any he ever tried before. He is given good clothing, set to do little jobs in a garden or on a road, which he accomplishes at the rate of employing the whole working day to do two hours' work. He is provided with good and regular food such as he cannot afford at home, and with delicacies he never dreamt of because he ignored them, or dreamt of vaguely because he had been told about them. In the meanwhile his women work the fields and get in his crop. When he leaves prison, fat and shiny, a cynosure for all eyes, admired by women and envied by men, instead of having to still pay at the least indemnity to the party he has injured, he will go home a happier and a richer man, to snigger at the law-abiding natives who sweat to pay taxes to maintain this extraordinary system. Of course the whites speak of the disgrace of prison, and of the sacrifice of personal liberty, as if they were deterrents. The natives listen to this solemnly, but they go back to their homes with their tongues in their cheeks and their thumbs to their noses at such ridiculous twaddle.

There is no doubt that white administration of justice, with its principle of education of the wrongdoer instead of punishment for crime, has made life far happier for the criminal in Africa than it was under native law. Proof of this is the multiplication of existing forms of crime and introduction of new ones so much deplored by those who knew the natives before and can compare the old days with the present.

In their disregard for every aspect of native life, the white man carelessly took no account of the fundamental difference separating the Christian from the Bantu philosophy; the former an exaltation of individualism, the latter of totalitarianism, both of them equally exigent and comprehensive in their demands while utterly irreconcilable in practice.

In Bantu tribal life the individualistic idea is simply non-existent, every member of the tribe, from the chief down to the lowest most insignificant individual, being a unit in an organic whole controlled by an ironbound code of duties, taboos and rights, upon the rigid observance of which tribal order and welfare depends. Every thought, every act of the people, from the moment that as infants they are definitely taken off their mother's backs at the end of weaning and set on their feet on the ground, to the hour of death, will be regulated by these orders. As babies they must first learn their own place in their mother's family, according to their sex, and then the status of their mother in a polygamous household. Extending from the household they must learn their position in the clan, by which is meant the complicated scale of relationships on both sides of the parent stock, and the distinctions of behaviour and of rights between paternal and maternal groups. Last of all the youth or the girl envisages the tribe, its customs and laws, none of which may be broken with impunity.

* * * * *

High tribute must be paid to the early missionaries in Africa, for their courage in braving the greatest dangers to further the glorious aims of spreading the Gospel and retrieve the natives from barbarism. Often the call would come to them suddenly to abandon the comforts of civilization, and to set out for distant lands to teach and preach among unappreciative savages. Gladly they would respond, gladly expose themselves to the perils of fever and wild beasts and the incredible deprivations of life there; patiently they would persevere through all trials, refusing to be discouraged, and willingly laying down their lives in the high service to which they had dedicated themselves.

Nevertheless, in spite of the highest aims and the noblest motives they blundered grievously.

THE BIRTH OF ETHIOPIANISM IN SOUTH AFRICA

They tackled problems they were not prepared to solve: they taught precepts they often could not put into practice themselves: they condemned customs they could not understand; lightly, and without reflecting upon the perils that might result. They gave exaggerated praise to converts in excess of their real merits, careless that in consequence these natives would regard themselves as superior to their pagan brethren. They deliberately aroused and appealed to a premature self-consciousness creating and fostering a non-existent nationalism as a spur to effort.

The fallacies of missionary teaching can roughly be divided under two headings: error in the religious field as towards the natives themselves, by the attempt to force Christianity on them in its legislative aspect rather than on abstract religious principles: error in the humanitarian and political sphere, regarded from the standpoint of racial aspirations, and social relations between black and white.

The spontaneous attitude of the tribes of South and Central Africa towards the white man was one of deep fear mingled with the humble conviction of their inferiority compared to the invader of their country, both sentiments richly tinged with dislike and hate. When they repelled the advances of friendly whites, and attacked or massacred them, it was out of fear of them, and in defence of the sanctuary of their homes, in order to keep out a disturbing influence, and hard and exacting taskmasters who could not be resisted once they were allowed to pass in. In the opposite case, when weak tribes made friendly submission to a handful of white men, and became obsequious to their commands, it was in blind and humble recognition of the authority of those few individuals, and of their power to protect them against other tribes stronger than their own which their consciousness told them could not hold up against the white man. There was never any doubt in their minds about the superiority of the white race.

To misplaced missionary zeal may safely be ascribed the responsibility of altering this wholesome outlook, probably as a consequence of the same blindness and conceit that characterized their conduct generally. One of the conditions of missionary concessions from all governments is that the missionaries will abstain from meddling in politics; a condition always accepted and never respected. In Africa this has been painfully evident and has had the most dismal effects.

One of the processes of evangelization is the inculcation in the native mind of the biblical theory of the equality of all men before God, to which no exception could be made if it had not implicitly included the equality of all men on earth also, of those who by the external physical facts of consenting to have a little cold water sprinkled on their woolly pates, of submitting to wearing

THE BIRTH OF ETHIOPIANISM IN SOUTH AFRICA

clothes they found uncomfortable and squeezing into boots that pinched their toes (discomforts as nothing compared with the rigour of their tribal initiation rites), of memorizing and gabbling off lessons said to be learnt by heart, but that certainly did not affect that organ, would be raised to the level of the white man. If, as has been said, the fault did not lie entirely with the missionaries, they cannot expect however to be exonerated from blame. For they never tried to resist the temptation of filling their churches and schools with undesirable material, or the glorious elation of surrounding themselves with crowds, eagerly listening to promises lightly made, irrespective of the chance of their being realized, or gave ever a thought to what would happen when their deluded pupils discovered they had been fooled.

As a corollary to the theory of equality, as a further spur to the acceptance of Christianity, the hitherto undreamt of ambition for self-expression and self-government was awakened; in other words the seed of nationalism was thoughtlessly sown and carefully cultivated.

It is beyond question that the responsibility for arousing prematurely sentiments and ambitions beyond the intelligence and development of primitive tribes lies with the missionaries, for these doctrines were maintained by them in the face of the disapproval of laymen whose knowledge of native language and psychology made them eminently capable of giving them timely warning of the folly of their ways, and the danger of deluding primitive and sensitive peoples with hopes bound to be crushed at the first contact with civilization. The missionaries were stubborn, deaf alike to arguments and protests, entrenching themselves behind the axiom that the Church does not accept advice from seculars, and that it knows its own business best. Indeed, opposition almost seemed to harden them in their resolution and they wantonly held on their way with unabated vigour, dinning into the ears of their pupils the glad tidings of equality, indifferent to the fact that in this particular they set as bad an example to the contrary as the majority of white men gave in the sphere of moral behaviour. For they did not deign to treat the dressed and Christianized natives, holders of school certificates or religious orders on a footing of equality either in intellectual, social or religious intercourse. And this their pupils resented fiercely, contending that man being vastly inferior to the Lord, if they could aspire to equality before the higher tribunal they were entitled to it before the lower. This break of faith offended them perhaps more bitterly than the laymen's hypocrisy in the matter of a moral code they officially and racially pretended to observe and uphold. They labelled this behaviour of the missionaries presumptuous and branded it as plain, unvarnished and un-

THE BIRTH OF ETHIOPIANISM IN SOUTH AFRICA

adulterated deceit, and a rank betrayal on the part of disciples of Christ. As polygamy was the stumbling-block of Christianity's moral code, so the fatuous admission of natives as recognized acolytes of the church positively paved the way for Christianity to become an instrument of revolt, rather than prepared the road to that universal brotherhood of man one is so wearyingly entertained with.

One might logically suppose that the outburst of nationalism would have provided the missionaries with matter for reflection they would not have dared to neglect. But only a chosen few agreed with the students of African psychology, that this amounted to a claim on the part of the natives to be invested with those rights of self-expression and self-government that had been put into their heads and hearts by the missionaries themselves; that the Ethiopianism they abused was an inevitable social movement bound to appear among peoples, once the artificially aroused consciousness of their value collided with the contradictions in the rule of the dominant race, at one and the same time continually demanding more of the natives and inciting them to further effort, while repressing any encroachment on their part.

The violent upsetting of all values and the forced abandonment of ancestral faiths and restraints did not prove advantageous to evangelization, nor did it bring about the anticipated improvement in moral outlook and discipline. It led instead to disintegration of the old order and introduced a rationalism and a general moral confusion whose fruits were disastrous. Not a single custom, not a single relationship, not a single traditional obligation escaped the interference of these fanatical spiritual directors, who cut the very ground from under the feet of their bewildered disciples, therefore frustrating even sincere and honest attempts to live the new life.

In particular, most pernicious effects were produced by the rigid exaction of monogamy and the scornful reviling of those natives who, out of a sense of justice or the affection of their hearts, refused to cast out wives and children from their kraals. It was neither wise nor equitable for the disappointed missionaries to condemn them as confirmed sensualists and to teach their children by implication, if not explicitly, to despise their parents as living in sin and being beyond the pale of redemption.

It is chiefly upon the rock of monogamy that Christianity founders. On the one hand the native sees no evidence in the Bible—the Christian book—for its enjoinment; on the other, the missionary makes no allowances for the social, economic and tribal foundations of polygamy. Monogamy in the kraal is in practice an impossibility, in a land where a woman cannot dispense with a man's protection; where she has no means of livelihood outside the kraal, where motherhood is a religious duty and an economic necessity, a native woman's first ambition and the justification of her existence; where union between man and wife are forbidden by religious taboos from the first signs of pregnancy to the end of the period of weaning—sometimes a matter of three or four or even more years. The missionaries, however, ignore all these considerations, identify polygamy with sexual excess, preach an extreme continence as the only path of salvation and the avenue to enlightenment, and demand rigid submission to monogamy from all who wish to enter the Church or remain within its precincts. They impose it as an insuperable condition of baptism in a drastic attempt to break down polygamy, forcing with hideous cruelty their converts to cut adrift all but one of their wives, bringing injustice, degradation and misery to thousands of respectable native women as worthless of consideration, although exemplary wives and mothers according to their own code and traditions. They are callous witnesses of the intense human suffering they are causing so long as they may save the souls of a small percentage of the men of a tribe. Is it unnatural that many of the native men out of their very manhood refuse complicity in such an outrage, repent them of hasty experiments and recall their discarded wives? Some instead make baptism a pretext to rid themselves of wives they have grown tired of, and later get in another set, causing endless strife over their broken tribal pledges. Besides it was a very grievous mistake to think that the natives would not take exception to the behaviour of the white men in general in Africa, of whom at one time 90 per cent were estimated to be "living in sin" with native women or to have intercourse with them, although many of them were known to have wives at home. The actual conduct of the white man as opposed to his official attitude could not escape the notice of the natives, who bitterly resented being called "renegades" or "dirty black savages" for acting in perfect accordance with the laws and customs of their country, by men who, while flagrantly transgressing their own vaunted laws and customs, yet demanded and obtained respect as individuals and Christians on the mere merit of their complexion.

It must in justice be granted that the missionaries on the spot continually had their hands forced by the associations at home that sent them out and provided for their maintenance, clamouring for immediate results with which to feed the enthusiasm of their supporters, confound their critics and set themselves up for the envy of their rivals. At no moment in history has the white man ever doubted his innate competence to judge what is good for the inferior coloured races, and when, about the middle of the nineteenth century, missionary activity put on a spurt it was inevitably influenced by the impracticable, ineradicable notions at home. There, Europeans with no conception or experience whatever of local problems, unable even faintly to imagine the actual conditions of native life in Africa, issued their fiats, based on the firmly held theoretical conviction that to civilize the native it was enough to send him to school from his earliest years, to give him a training designed to substitute wholesale the white man's moral principles for the black man's so-called superstitions and atavistic traditions. They argued that they had only to put down a set of regulations comprehensive enough and detailed enough to govern every contingency of a native's life, every thought and gesture for evermore.

On this sophistry missionary endeavour at this time was based, and bore its inevitable fruits of disappointment, confusion, embitterment and moral anarchy. Each year the missionary who wished to be considered a success strove to report a growing number of catechumens, of conversions, of pupils at his school, and most direful of all, of native ministers.[1] Otherwise he was liable to be rebuked and recalled in disgrace. Therefore he held mass baptisms and opened school after school without sufficiently reflecting on the type of curriculum best adapted to the

[1] Appendix I. The statistic of Jesuits in one province of Congo Belge.

native mind. The natives were given set lessons to learn, and to the wonder and delight of their teachers absorbed with the greatest facility all that was laid before them. Their marvellous memories and quick imitativeness enabled them to learn by rote without really assimilating the content and to ape white customs without modifying in any way their fundamental disposition. It has taken the white man over half a century to realize the astonishing retentiveness of the fresh African brain and to grasp the fact that the native's amazing facility for memorizing the white man's words is mere psittacism, merely labial repetition which neither penetrates the mind nor influences the conduct of the learner. When he returns to the kraal he throws off and despises the white garment of civilization which he seemed to have worn so naturally and openly resumes his native customs and habits of thought. Even today, in the fourth generation of schoolgoers, careful observation reveals the same characteristics that so easily mislead the inexperienced.

For their part, the natives flocked and still flock to the schools independently of any religious motive. They clamour for an education which they fondly believe and are cruelly encouraged by the whites to believe, will raise them forthwith to the white man's level. As for the restrictions and obligations of Christianity, these they accept as troublesome details incidental to their great ambition of a white man's education. While they are in the school they will usually profess conversion in order better to exploit the opportunities which the mission school offers them, but when the time comes for them to return to their kraals and take their places in tribal life, they renounce their superficial and temporary Christianity without compunction, and indifferent to the fact that they will be branded as renegades by the missionaries. For in the view of the best natives the Christian convert is an apostate to the creed of his fathers, a traitor to his tradition, without reverence for tribal authority or respect for tribal moral codes, a degenerate discarding every ideal of tribal virtue. For too often the young convert jumps at Christianity because it affords him an escape from the onerous and painful duties which his position in the tribe entails. The young undisciplined members of the tribe wishing to escape tribal control early learn that they can pit the authority of the magistrate and the missionary against that of the chief and vice versa. They become past-masters at the game, brazenly turning from one to the other as it suits their own purpose, and as a rule they will profess Christianity when it suits them, to evade tribal duties and tributes, and refer to native custom they no longer observe as an excuse to the magistrate in order to justify some misdemeanour and plead for and obtain a sentence lighter by far than the one they could expect if judged by the law of the tribe.

Real Christianity cannot be said to have made much progress among the Bantu people. In many districts where missionary effort has worked for nearly a century, the percentage of the population that affects Christianity at all after leaving school does not exceed 12 per cent, while many sincere missionaries are obliged ruefully to admit a much lower percentage, 8 per cent or 5 per cent. One missionary with a professed community of 5,000, on being asked "How many real believers in Christ and a future life would you point out in your flock, people really striving to live up to His teachings?" replied with tears in his eyes, "Not one. May the Lord deal with me for what I have striven to do and not by my failure, or I have given up my life in vain." Nor was he the only one to reply in that manner. Others, more fortunate, may have a few. In the first rush a certain number of chiefs, attracted by the glitter of Christianity and flattered by the attentions of the missionaries consented to be baptized; but during the last decades they have been steadily falling away. At one time there were several Zulu chiefs Christians in name if not in fact; today there are none. In other tribes the same thing has happened, and it is in fact practically impossible for a chief to be a Christian. They rapidly ascertained that as Christians they could not rule the tribe,

THE BIRTH OF ETHIOPIANISM IN SOUTH AFRICA

just as well as the tribes have awoken to the fact that they cannot possibly get on with a Christian chief. In one of the large mission schools of the Transkei in 1933, the son of a chief, succumbing to his environment, asked for baptism, but he was warned by his tribe that if he took that step he would forfeit his heirdom.

For a variety of reasons Christianity appealed to unworthy elements in a tribe; for the opportunities it held out to the ambitious, the restless, the lovers of personal aggrandizement and self-glorification. It had the power of attracting the class of people that under the old order took up witch-doctoring as the only career able to satisfy these hungers. For the black man shares his white brother's gnawing desire for publicity and authority; he also aspires to prominence and the ministry gave him just this scope for exhorting, arraigning, bewailing, invoking, threatening, cursing, that gratified his deepest emotions. The Bantu natives, however ignorant they may appear by European standards, are anything but fools, and have an ingrained inherent mysticism, which is finely developed by their tradition and training. They will credit any story and believe in it implicitly, yet they are shrewd, wily, subtle rationalists, resourceful in discussion, fertile in deduction, with a veritable genius for logomachy. Argumentation is pure delight to them and the sheer verbosity of Christianity, its prayers, its

THE SEETHING AFRICAN POT

readings, its preachings, its singing, were in themselves a lure for the intelligent.

But even when the natives adopted Christianity, especially when they attained the rank of the ministry, they found its rules too difficult to put in practice and to live up to, on the lines laid down for them by the whites, and demanded the right to adapt it to their own environment, and yet be recognized as Christians and be entitled to respect as such.

* * * * *

The first little shoot of active discontent appeared in 1882 in Tembuland, when a native Wesleyan minister called Tile, his pride frayed more than usual by some petty incident, broke from his mission alleging that he could by himself satisfy all the demands of his flock. He set up an independent native religious association of which nothing is known, except that it was not crowned with any notable success, and quickly fizzled out.

Seven years later, in 1889, there arrived at one of the Berlin missions among the BaPedi a new recruit called Winter who was a typical example of the rash, over-sympathetic, over-zealous, headstrong white equalitarian who easily does so much mischief. Immediately upon his arrival, before he had gained knowledge of his work, or experience of the natives, he jumped to the conclusion that the whites in general, and his own colleagues in the mission in particular, were too standoffish with the blacks. "We ought to treat our flock not as inferiors, but as equals," he declared, "at any rate those natives who are Christians and have certificates of schooling." Whether out of irresponsibility, or from the desire to make a bid for cheap popularity with the natives, Winter proclaimed his views openly among them. They met of course with enthusiastic approval, and on the eager proposal of one of the native ministers who had pushed himself into the van of the movement, Winter set up an independent native church. The first decision of the vestry on taking office was to dismiss Winter as an interloper, which may have opened his eyes to the folly of his action, but by then the mischief was done and the fatal precedent created.

News travels fast in Africa without mechanical aids, and that same year in Pretoria, a native minister called Kenyane, belonging to a Mission, availed himself of the opportunity afforded by the absence of his bishop on holiday in England to organize an independent black community which he persuaded his whole congregation to join, refusing when summoned, to return to his allegiance to the white missionaries, but not otherwise causing any trouble.

It was not until four years later, in 1893, that the first serious crisis occurred on the occasion of a missionary congress held at Pretoria, at which the initial mistake of asking the native ministers to join at all was made. Further, the invitation was issued in identical terms with that for the whites, so that the native ministers arrived with the preconceived expectation of being given an equal standing with the white ones. Instead they found themselves wholly excluded from the board of the congress and with no representation in the direction of its activities. This angered them considerably, and when at its first sitting the board resolved that the representatives of the two races should meet separately, and further, that while black meetings should be open to the whites, reciprocity was denied and the white meetings were closed to the blacks, they were furious.

Boiling with rage at what they proclaimed to be an insult, the native ministers withdrew in a body from the congress and held outside protest meetings where they gave vent to their wrath in no measured terms. They threw the Christian doctrine of the equality of all men before God in the teeth of their opponents, protesting against the monstrous and absurd inconsistency of differentiating unequally between black and white ministers of the very gospel of equality which it was their joint task to respect. They feverishly searched the Bible for bolts to hurl at the arrogant whites, and the book which had been placed in their raw hands before they were mature enough to use it now became a weapon to be turned against their quondam teachers.

THE BIRTH OF ETHIOPIANISM IN SOUTH AFRICA

It was at this point that the agitation among the South African Christian natives began to show the repercussion of a contemporary agitation that was going on among the negroes of U.S.A. Indeed, the South African movement probably was a distant echo of the American negro racial movement, one of whose favourite and recent theories was that the original tribes from which they were drawn were descendants of the Ethiopians. It was a theory not only without any scientific basis but also in direct antithesis with all Bantu traditions and folklore, but it had caught the fancy of the American negroes and they had adopted it eagerly.

It is hardly surprising, in view of the constant intercourse between America and South Africa, that the fancy of the American negroes should have reached the ears of a few of the Africans, and somehow it had come to the knowledge of Mokone, a deputy at the Pretoria congress and one of the most rabid champions of the rights and dignity of the native ministers. He handed it on to his companions who instantly seized upon it as presenting that very synthesis for which they had been searching. Ethiopianism, fortuitous as it was, provided them with a peg on which to hang their discontent and offered them a positive formula embodying a conception soothing to their pride. And thus, suddenly and irrationally, the disaffected South Africans also switched their thoughts to Ethiopia, a country the very existence of which many had ignored till that moment, with which they had neither bond of blood nor of tradition, neither a common language nor a common religion, bewailing themselves as her miserable children, hailing her as their long-lost mother and calling upon her to clasp them to her ample bosom and deliver them from the white man's bondage and tyranny. In earnest of the sincerity of their devotion a dissentient native church dedicated to their remote and imaginary ancestress was founded. It was the first church of the "Ethiopian" denomination, probably the still existing "Ethiopian Church Lamentation of South Africa," although it is almost impossible after the lapse of so many years to be quite certain of the order of precedence among the various Ethiopian church denominations in South Africa. Nor does it very much matter.

II THE GROWTH OF ETHIOPIANISM IN AFRICA

The mutinous native ministers of Pretoria had seized upon the catchword of Ethiopianism with hysterical eagerness and delight, finding in it something really corresponding to their racial yearnings, but they were too raw and inexperienced to know how to translate it into a working formula, or how to build up any effective machinery of revolt. Therefore, on the dispersal of the congress, the movement subsided into a complete and inglorious obscurity with only Mokone and a little band of followers to nourish the germ of the new faith and save it from extinction.

Then in 1896 the movement was infused with new and startling vitality in an unforeseen manner owing to another error of judgment on the part of white missionaries, who had received Mokone's outburst flippantly, covering it with a mixture of ridicule and vituperation hardly conducive to a healing of the breach, and confirming that lack of comprehension of native psychology which has already been commented on.

A Wesleyan mission, being sadly in need of

funds, conceived the notion of sending one of its best pupils to England, hoping, by presenting an example of the efficiency of their methods, to induce an unimaginative and niggardly public to relax its purse-strings. It chose one of the native ministers, James Duwane, who had been ordained since 1881, whose behaviour had been exemplary for the intervening fifteen years, whose work had been beyond praise, and devotion beyond question. In him the mission centred its hopes; he was dispatched on his errand with affectionate valedictions, and in full confidence that he would arouse interest and achieve the purpose entrusted to him.

Nor were the missionaries mistaken. Duwane took London by storm. He was lionized, praised, petted, acclaimed and entertained until the memory of his past life faded like a bad dream. No longer was he the humble native who stood in the rain shivering at the back door awaiting his master's orders, or at most venturing into the kitchen, ranking less than the dog who shared his master's room and food. In London he was invited to meet the whites on equal terms; he entered their houses by the front door, shook hands with them in friendship, sat down at table with them. The consciousness of a new dignity of manhood and citizenship dawned on him, and his heart opened to a new sense of brotherly love and equality towards those before whom he had previously held himself in lowly self-abasement, regarding it as an honour if they wiped their shoes upon him. Duwane was a changed man and the bearer of high compliments to his mission and affectionate and encouraging messages to his own people when he returned to his ship, his head in the clouds, proud of his performance, confident in his newly-found dignity, hopeful beyond bounds for the future of his race.

Alas for Duwane! His triumph was brief. On reaching his ship he was brought down to earth again with a bang that left him dazed. No longer was he the respected member of society, an admired and petted friend, but once more a "dam' nigger" to be kicked and sworn at by the lowest of whites. The happy world he had built up in England crumbled about him as it has crumbled for thousands of coloured people before and since. Those who have never experienced it cannot realize the fury, the hatred, the rebelliousness which this cruelty engenders. It would be far kinder, and even more just, to maintain the policy of racial prejudice in Europe than to delude its unfortunate victims into the belief that the friendship which they have received in Europe on their own merits can be extended to them on the same principles in their native land.

In his humiliation and disgust Duwane reacted violently from what he felt to be an injustice and an outrage. His love changed to hatred, his friendship into the bitterest enmity, his pride to gall; he turned against the very teachers he had previously revered, seeing in them oppressors disdainfully holding down the blacks in a hateful tutelage. He stepped off the ship obsessed with the idea of raising his brothers to a position of independence, of freeing them from the bondage of the whites and of giving them religious autonomy. His first step on landing was to renounce his mission and to seek out Mokone. His superior training enabled him to see at a glance that Mokone's struggling community would never prosper unless a firmer hand took the helm. That he made no attempt to suggest himself as a pilot to the frail bark shows both his intelligence and his outstanding sincerity, for few natives can resist the temptation to assert themselves. He was the odd man in a million not to have claimed the leadership as his right. In England he had learnt much about the vindication campaign of the American negroes and its rapidly acquired strength, and he now suggested an alliance with the transatlantic organization.

The proposal was met with unqualified favour, funds were hastily collected, and for the second time Duwane crossed the ocean on an embassy, this time very different from the preceding one, as he prepared to lay the troubles of the Africans of Africa before the Africans of America and implore aid from the more advanced brethren. He was supported by a brother dissenting native minister called Xaba, of whom nothing more is known.

This American movement was started in 1787 by some negroes taking exception to being restricted to the back seats in chapel and being kept waiting for Communion until all the whites present had been attended to. Tentative separate black communities were formed; the innovation met with the warmest approval from all the negroes, and black independent churches sprang up all over the land. In 1816 several of these churches were incorporated in a vast organization that by 1890 counted about 500,000 members under eleven bishops. They were more or less divided into two principal bodies calling themselves respectively Baptists and Methodists and cultivating hatred for their former masters much more energetically than any Christian virtue.

Early in the nineties a religious association taking the name of the Watchtower was started by the white Methodist Church to promote in the name of Jesus Christ universal brotherhood and the equality of the races. The negroes had joined it practically *en masse*, and it was to this Watchtower Association that Duwane and Xaba appealed for support in the name of their common African Mother.

The reception accorded to the two African envoys by the emotional negroes of America surpassed their highest hopes, and the negroes of the

THE SEETHING AFRICAN POT

Watchtower Association immediately decided to send out to Africa one of their leading men, Bishop Turner, a pillar of the Society, to assist the more primitive natives and to put the African Ethiopian movement on its feet.

Bishop Turner was welcomed by the South African natives with delirious enthusiasm and with an acclamation that could hardly have been more unrestrained had he been the Messiah. Indeed, posing as he did as the liberator of the African peoples, he was almost certainly confounded by many of the more ignorant natives with the Saviour himself—to the infinite amusement and unbridled scorn of the whites.

However, Turner was a thinker and knew both his subject and his public. And when he fired the country with his flaming oratory, belching forth like a volcano in full eruption, exploding like a lighted powder-magazine, he sent the natives wild with hysterical exultation and filled the whites with alarm. He expounded the Ethiopian doctrine that had so powerfully captivated the American negroes, developing its ideals and aims from the same text, the thirty-first verse of Psalm LXVIII. As it had roused the nationalism of the Americans, it now stirred that of the Africans:

"Princes shall come out of Egypt; Ethiopia shall soon stretch out her hands to God."

He gave his hearers good, stimulating orations, appealing to their vanity and ambition, holding up to scorn those who affirmed that the blacks were a decadent race, recalling the past greatness of Ethiopia, boldly expounding the descent of the Xosa peoples from this alien parent stock, prophesying the advent of the black races on a day soon to dawn, whenever they shook off their long sleep to rise to irresistible power and rule over the land of their forefathers. He painted for them a stirring picture of Ethiopia, the Great African Mother, holding out her arms to God to invoke his blessing. He rhetorically merged Ethiopia into all Africa, all Africa into Ethiopia, and set up the cry of "Africa for the Africans," which became their slogan, and which has never died down to this day in spite of the many modifications of its intentions. Turner perhaps rather let his fancy run away with him when he traced Xosa descent right up to Kush, a piece of information that stuck in their throats before being swallowed, and never was really digested.

"Why has the white man's civilization contributed so little to the advancement of the African?" yelled the bishop. "It is because the white man does not appreciate our value, because he believes himself by divine right to be the dominant race and thereby privileged to maintain all the others in a state of subordination. The black is the race of the future, and one day the black man will wake up and shake off the white man's yoke. He is already rubbing his eyes and feeling his muscles."

THE SEETHING AFRICAN POT

Galvanized out of their unconcern the missionaries retorted by reminding the natives how much they owed to them, and comparing their conditions generally to what their life had been before the white man arrived in Africa.

Bishop Turner had a neat tongue for controversy. He examined the reasons for which the South Africans had remained savages in spite of white missionaries, whose efforts he granted as noble, but too restricted and clogged by racial prejudices to give the evangelization of Africa the necessary impulse.

"The time has now come to replace them, with their antiquated methods and superannuated principles. Our new doctrine," he affirmed, "is more suited to the African awakening, and *only the sons of New Africa may be trusted to propagate it, not any aliens.* Africa," roared the bishop, "is a new land, a new world; she needs new men, and we are the men she needs. Arise, Africa! for Ethiopia is holding out her arms, not as a suppliant, as the white men call her, but to incite us to throw out our arms like boxers, seize the enemy, chuck him out and conquer the first place among peoples."

On this basis Turner inaugurated Ethiopianism as a national movement, with a free church. He ordained two thousand native ministers and ordered them to go and proclaim his gospel far and wide. His disciples obeyed his injunctions literally, rushing through the territories now included in the Union of South Africa, the

THE GROWTH OF ETHIOPIANISM IN AFRICA

British Protectorates of Swaziland, Basutoland and Bechuanaland, through the two Rhodesias, Tanganyika, Uganda, Kenya, the Portuguese, Belgian and French colonies. In a couple of years the whole of the Bantu tribes, from the Cape of Good Hope to the Equator, and a little beyond it, were overrun with native ministers whose progress was marked by the dissenting native churches that sprang up everywhere. To these were given various and amazing denominations; several were dedicated to the Ethiopian Mother, a very few to the Kushite ideal, but they all professed the African's creed that he had the right to mould Christianity to a form more suited to his traditions and to enjoy ecclesiastical autonomy.

Within the Union of South Africa there are today 272 denominations of native dissident churches registered by the Government.[1] Of these there are twenty-one of the Ethiopian variety, such as the already-mentioned Ethiopian Church Lamentation of South Africa—the African Ethiopian Church—the Abyssinian Baptist Church—the Ethiopian Church of Basutoland—the Church of Abyssinia—the Gazaland Zimbabwe Ethiopian Church—the Bechuana Metho-

---

[1] Appendix III. Official list of native churches recognized by the Government of the Union of South Africa, published in *Modern Industry and the African* by kind permission of the Editor, J. Merle Davis, and of the publishers, Messrs. Macmillan.

dist in Zion Church—the National Church of Ethiopia in South Africa—the Zulu Ethiopian Church—the National Swazi Native Apostolic Church of Africa, etc., besides the Kush Nineveh Church and the Kush Apostolic Church. This list does not comprise the native churches registered outside the Union, which are estimated by well-informed people to bring the number to at least four hundred, nor the unregistered ones, which are legion.

After having described how Ethiopianism owed its inception to the frayed pride and thwarted ambition of a handful of enraged native ministers, it is time to examine its popularity with the masses in order to understand its headlong rush through a vast area of Africa. The mere fact that Christianity under white propaganda proceeded slowly on its painful way, while under native guidance Ethiopianism advanced by leaps and bounds, though only nascent and still unable to express itself, offers food for thought.

The appeal to a tangible deity would have been enthusiastically welcomed by the Bantu tribes, for it went straight to their emotional hearts. The embodiment of Christian doctrine in a God, Lord or Master corresponded almost directly with their own timid and ill-defined conception of N'Kos, also Lord and Master, a mystical figure never mentioned but dimly apprehended as a Supreme Being existing in a remote and unspecified sphere, possibly beyond the sky. In their extreme humility the Bantu dare not invoke this Being directly either in prayer or in sacrificial ceremonies; all these are addressed to the spirits of their ancestors whose duty it is to intercede with N'Kos [1] for such of their descendants on earth as remember them with offerings. This belief is apparently subconscious and implied, for in the prayers, invocations and sacrifices which are addressed to the spirits of the ancestors, no explicit mention of intercession on behalf of their petitions is ever audibly made.

The Bantu conception of a future life is very rudimentary. At death the spirit of the departed must be presented to those of preceding ancestors by means of animal sacrifice, and it survives only as long as there are direct descendants of the body to keep it, through the medium of these ceremonies, attached to the earth. Therefore children of the body are a primary complement of Bantu religions, and that is the reason why those women who are overlooked in legal marriage fall back on concubinage or free union as the only means of bearing a child, and are not dishonoured by doing so, as they must provide for their souls. For the spirits of the childless will join the legion of the unworshipped ones and sink into a vague limbo of forgotten spirits. (As a matter of fact there is also the economic factor, as in primitive life

[1] The name may vary among different tribes.

THE SEETHING AFRICAN POT

having a child means literally providing for one's old age.)

A God who can be addressed personally and directly, though rather awe-inspiring, is nevertheless a Deity of great attraction. The representation of the Deity as a sole figure, or in a Trinity, or with the addition of a Queen of the Heavens, is a matter of supreme indifference to them. They are ready to believe any number of tales of the sort, the more the merrier. The incarnation of the Deity in the form of an earthly Son is also accepted without demur, all miracles, by whomsoever performed, are believed in literally, and white missionaries are often confused with witch-doctors by the natives, as purveyors of ultrapotent and fascinating charms. Several of the miracles of Jesus, especially the raising of the dead and the healing of the sick, are very commonly staged by the Black Prophets, as these native ministers are called in Africa who are endowed with a gift of expression and suddenly get divine inspiration and start a seditious following.

The opposition to Christianity, it is necessary to repeat even at the cost of becoming tedious, came from its inadaptability to the traditions and customs of the primitive Bantu tribes, and the strength of Ethiopianism lies in its clever if unorthodox reconciliation of Christian doctrines with them.

First of all Ethiopianism sanctioned polygamy

on the ground that the Patriarchs and other leading personages of the Bible, the Book of Books for Christianity, often had a plurality of wives without being discredited for it, and deduced from this that the intransigence of the white missionaries who exacted monogamy as a *sine qua non* of admittance to the Church was merely lamentable obtuseness and not justified on the Bible's own showing, which in itself gave the natives every right to follow their temperament and customs.

On practically the same lines Ethiopianism disposed of the Church's opposition to ancestor-worship, insisting that there was no discrepancy in reconciling Christianity with it. In all forms of Christianity the principle of vicarious intercession is accepted, through the mediation of the Saviour, and by the Roman Catholics is extended to a phalanx of saints; if the Deity could be addressed by the saints, it was argued, and could listen to their intercessions, all the more were the spirits of their ancestors likely to be heard, as they would have a more personal interest in transmitting the desires of their descendants than mere strangers assailed by requests from all sides. Furthermore, by this arrangement the spirits of the ancestors who had departed before the advent of Christianity would thereby profit by the transaction, for in providing for the welfare of their descendants they would find the opportunity of maintaining their contact with the earth.

The problem of witchcraft was dismissed with similar reasonings. Granting that the miracles of Christ should be kept in a class reserved to Messiahs òn grounds of divinity, what of those of all the saints, who during their lifetime had been plain, ordinary men and women like themselves? They surely could not be entitled to the same respect as those of the Deity, and by the natives were uniformly classified as witchcraft. For Moses they have a special veneration, admiring both his qualities of leadership and his miracles. To them he is one of the greatest exponents of witchcraft in his medianic powers of providing food and water, and in his direct intercourse with the Deity, as when he received the Tables of the Law. Ethiopians further accord him their gratitude on account of the noble defence of his Ethiopian wife.

Yet, apart from its theological aspect, a matter better left to ecclesiastical discussion, it were futile to decry the humanity of the native dissident churches. By eliminating, with casuistical jugglery, the drawbacks to the newly-discovered ideology of Christianity, they brought the creed within reach not only of the men, but also of the women of the tribes, those piteous victims of white evangelization, and from the old grandmother grieving for daughter and granddaughter, down to the young girl fearful of her fate when her turn came to be married, they one and all

THE GROWTH OF ETHIOPIANISM IN AFRICA

supported it. This much must be said for it: the native dissident church opened its arms wide to all and sundry, without leaving a wake of heart-burnings and distress.

There is a certain danger that this explanation may be misleading, for one might reasonably deduce from it that the whole native population was satisfied with this modified form of Christianity and had adopted it. Only an incredibly long examination of the depth of their religious beliefs and superstitions and their attachment to their cherished customs could even superficially explain the complex reasons which caused the superior-minded natives to remain faithful to their old traditions and beliefs, for even in its modified form it appealed to the malcontents and the undisciplined. Therefore, notwithstanding that Ethiopianism collected a following of hundreds of thousands of disaffected natives, they are as nothing compared to the millions who have shunned it.

Further, it may be of interest to note, though not pertinent to the subject under examination, that many African tribes who had lived for centuries in touch with Mohammedanism without being affected by it, have as a reaction against missionary pressure passed to it in a body. There are instances of this recorded time and again in Central Africa, and it is an indisputable fact that excessive missionary zeal has enormously con-

THE SEETHING AFRICAN POT

tributed to the propagation of an antagonistic faith, positively preparing the way for its triumphal march throughout the Continent.

* * * * *

After the culminating ceremonies of ordination, in which he saw the completion of his task, Bishop Turner had gone back to his own diocese in America, and the nascent Ethiopian movement was left to its own devices. The first rush of enthusiasm over, the native ministers found themselves quite at a loss how to proceed, and were further dismayed by the then Cape Government's refusal to sanction their ordination.

In its fanatical race through the land the Ethiopian movement had swept every type of recruit into its ranks. Had it retained its first genuine patriotic and religious character, it might have represented a crucible in which the latent gold of the tribes might have burnt pure. But in its hasty indiscriminativeness it began to embrace men and women of inferior calibre, without spiritual idealism, whose worst rather than their best passions were inflamed by the general fervour, whose ardour was but a cloak for their vanity, and whose adherence ministered only to their longing for power and their instinctive demagogy.

Deprived of Turner's authority, the leadership of the movement fell vacant with nobody strong enough to fill it; to the great relief of the whites, who had looked upon this schism with extreme displeasure and huge scorn. Openly they had jeered at it and piled contempt upon it, predicting for the most part that it would quickly fade, well knowing the inaptitude of the natives for continual exertion and their congenital frailty before financial temptation.

Their predictions were apparently to be fulfilled. Bickerings and squabblings of an infinitely indecorous kind broke out in the serried ranks of Ethiopianism, whose army decayed and disbanded almost as quickly as a couple of years before it had formed itself in a veritably insensate devotion. Even Duwane and Mokone fell out, and rumour has it that the former, the only South African native bishop of the time whose name is recorded, disgusted by what he judged a betrayal of his comrades, attempted a reconciliation with the Wesleyan mission which he had previously deserted. Finding the door slammed in his face he then tried his luck with a Roman Catholic mission, with the same result.

The missionaries rubbed their hands and congratulated themselves on the second collapse of Ethiopianism, on the whole being unable to detect that little centres of revolt, tiny seeds fallen in fertile soil, still flourished all over the land, carrying on a furtive guerilla warfare against white missionary evangelization and keeping alive a spark that might kindle another conflagration at a favourable opportunity.

THE SEETHING AFRICAN POT

News of the failure of Ethiopianism's second flight in Africa soon reached America together with a renewed petition for help and an assurance that a hidden torch saved the sacred flame from extinction. A meeting of the Watchtower was called to discuss the situation, at which Bishop Turner expatiated at length on the futility of expecting such primitive people to keep running the machinery of so complicated an enterprise. He now confessed that he had been struck at his first encounter by the mediocrity of the men to whom a task far beyond their intellectual maturity had been allotted. He had however purposely refrained from expressing his doubts of their capability in order not to damp their ardour. Besides, he had expected more from Duwane and Mokone.

In the face of the present crisis he maintained the necessity of keeping the direction of the movement in the hands of the Watchtower if Ethiopianism were to be given another chance. Otherwise it would, like any venture left in the hands of the South African natives, blaze up for a moment and end again in an absurd exhibition. Remembering the hostility of the whites, he recommended the avoidance of all publicity, enjoining secrecy as indispensable to success. His advice was taken *in toto*, and a motion was passed that the Watchtower should send out its own agents to various places in Africa with specific instructions which were to be modified according to the progress that was made.

It would take too long to examine in detail the activities of the agents, black and white, their gradual infiltration among the natives, slowly but surely extending their sphere of influence. Usually the black preachers were sent to make direct contact with the natives while, in the beginning at least, the white agents remained more in the background, in a fiduciary capacity, directing affairs and reporting on developments, offering suggestions, etc. Made wary by their earlier experiences the agents proceeded cautiously, insinuating themselves into the tribes as the chance arose of doing so without exciting the suspicion of the authorities. They arrived with none of the ostentation that had marked Bishop Turner's movements, but settled down quietly to work, beginning in the Cape Province, the birthplace of the previous Ethiopian Crusade.

* * * * *

One might logically suppose that the outbreak of Ethiopianism would have convinced the white section of the population of the necessity of carefully investigating its causes and meticulously analysing its designs, however unpalatable it might be. Instead, the attitude of the whites in this unpleasant crisis in their lives is sincerely to be deplored, for it was totally unsympathetic towards the new aspirations and met them with withering contempt, in a blind fury with the natives for daring to voice their grievances, indeed, for daring to have any grievances at all. Perhaps, if this paroxysm of patriotism and religious fervour had been studied at the time and been placed under a wise and tactful guidance, it might have been the means of establishing a beneficent restraint upon, and of securing a hold over the more effervescent class of the native population. Its first effect, beyond widening the already existing gulf between the two races, was the amazing one of setting the various white classes at loggerheads with each other. On the whole, it can be said that the laymen turned in a body against the missionaries, saddling them with the responsibility for the commotion. This unkind criticism the missionaries deeply resented, already smarting as they were with discomfiture at the unforeseen turn of events, and at the recoil from standards they had deluded themselves into believing were firmly established. They retorted in no measured terms, upholding the righteousness of their teachings and switching the blame back on to the shoulders of the laymen.

Both sides were completely blinded by the beams in their respective eyes and in the heat of discussion some very nasty, rash and silly things were said on both sides, that might well have been left unsaid. Matters became far worse when in the missionary field there appeared a rift within the lute, as the representatives of rival churches and denominations fell on each other tooth and nail. Instead of sanely reviewing the situation and joining forces to meet it, they descended to incredible depths, exchanging cheap recriminations and stinging accusations, momentarily oblivious of the ninth commandment and devoid of the brotherly love they discoursed on so glibly from the pulpit. Apparently believing themselves absolved from observance of elementary rules of politeness in virtue of their devotion to their cause, they exchanged apostolic blows and evangelical anathemas in terms so cogent that from any less saintly source they would have been called vulgar in the extreme; a deplorable practice that prevails to this day, and is detrimental not only to their personal prestige but to that of the white man in general and to religion in particular. Both laymen and ecclesiastics, in the general friction, forgot the issues at stake and neglected to examine the omens apodeictically foretelling calamitous events. Characteristically they agreed on momentous errors, as chiefly: the inaptitude of the natives for sustained effort or for keeping secrets; their fickleness, impracticability, lack of determination. Racial prejudice blinding them, they continued for years without seeing whither Ethiopianism trended, obstinately stiffening in the fatuous conviction that each riot was the isolated effluxion of local extremists, steadily refusing to recognize it as a thread of a fabric being woven over the whole country.

At this juncture a third party appeared upon the scene, quite a small group of thinkers, also a mixture of laymen and ecclesiastics, who by their discriminating insight and their intimacy with the natives, due to direct contact with them and their knowledge of the vernacular, had a wider outlook, and could better estimate the situation at its real importance. These people sounded the tocsin of alarm and made themselves thoroughly unpopular with both contending groups by impartially ascribing the responsibility to them equally. On one hand they gave the missionaries a severe trouncing for mixing sweet sentimentality and humanitarian drivel with reprehensible demagogy, admonishing them to beware of facile baptisms and to cease from vitiated reasonings and vapourings ill adapted to primitive peoples. Gravely concerned with the unfairness of stuffing the natives with nonsensical doctrines on one day, and denying the effects of their precepts on the morrow, they adjured them simultaneously to deflect their teaching into a saner channel, and to reconsider the cruelty of giving the natives an illusory higher education they had no use for in their lives, while neglecting other branches of learning that would benefit them.

The missionary mind works in a curious way, for even at the height of dissension, and in face of the conflagration, they refused stubbornly to listen to reason or accept advice, denying that their training of the natives was at fault or warranted rebuke, and clinging to it chapter and verse on an unchanging course.

On the other hand the laymen came in for their full share of the blame; not only their misdemeanours and their antipathy towards the natives were upheld to the public gaze, but they were severely rated for misrepresenting the value of the movement, for belittling its causes and the qualities of the natives, and for refusing to take any steps towards controlling it. All this small group derived from the warnings they gave was the satisfaction of a duty accomplished against overwhelming odds, for they aroused the opposition of the great majority of the whites, who actually managed to patch up a sort of truce between themselves in order to cry them down as alarmists and cowardly dodderheads. This adverse criticism did not disturb them at all, and their numbers slowly increased as time went by.

Through all these intervening years, these parties have maintained their characteristic attitude unchanged, the natives as well as the whites, and the situation has steadily grown worse from day to day and from year to year, aggravated by the heritage of hate each rebellion and each riot has left behind it. Nor has the white man in Europe taken more than a superficial or fleeting interest in events so nearly concerning him though occurring in a far distant quarter of the globe. The best example of this indifference is given by the excitement caused by the articles of Senator Coty in *L' Ami de Peuple*, for they raised a violent controversy which died down quickly as nearer and apparently more pressing affairs demanded attention. Thus the storm has gathered momentum and each time it breaks it makes the past occasions seem as squalls by comparison.

* * * * *

Ecclesiastical independence and a modified Christianity had been the limit of the original demands of Ethiopianism; but once the intervention of the American negroes had been obtained and their leadership established, its trend in Africa had to follow on the trail blazed for it by them. So that as soon as the Watchtower took over control in Africa, Ethiopianism changed its outlook, for the American negroes by that time had already passed the initial stages, and were provided with a full ecclesiastical hierarchy, and the question of religious independence was definitely superseded by that of equality with the whites in all fields, under the auspices of a dawning socialism. When socialism took possession of the U.S.A. early in this century, gaining a large following of white proletarians, the American negroes joined whole-heartedly a movement so very much to their taste, rapturously flattered by the realization of what had once seemed a forlorn hope, namely that of belonging to a political white body on a footing of equality with its less richly pigmented members.

In 1914 a Negro Student Conference met in Atalanta, from May 14th to 18th, attended by 665 delegates, of whom only 70 were white and 595 coloured. There were 470 students, and the remainder were sympathizers.

The subject under discussion was how to give the present generation of negro students in the U.S.A. their responsibility for leadership in Christian work at home and abroad—"to face the responsibility resting upon the negro churches of America, to help the claims and crises of Africa, and to consider what light Christian thought may throw on present and future co-operation between the races." But the student delegates and their white friends, people honestly convinced of having been singled out by the Almighty to be philosophic fugitives from hidebound and antiquated schools of thought, were much more concerned with the Church in its relation to negro problems and the question of the American negro's responsibility for African missions.

At the end a motion was passed:

"Three centuries of life in the U.S.A. had advanced the negro's average attainment far beyond that of his African contemporaries, while his racial consciousness

THE SEETHING AFRICAN POT

can interpret more truly than others the needs of his primitive brethren. He embodies in the representative young men and women of his people here the goal after which Africa should strive."

The result of the Conference was a sort of mass emigration of propagandists from America to Africa, followed by an increase of the number of young Bantu sent to America and Europe to High School and Universities, with the object of their coming into direct contact with modern thought. Under the care of the delegates of the Watchtower this side of the question that had been introduced to the Africans by Bishop Turner was assiduously developed, and the slogan "Africa for the Africans" no longer signified religious autonomy alone, but enlarged its scope to include complete equality with the whites in all fields, cultural, social, intellectual and commercial. The blacks of Africa were assured that they deserved it in virtue of the examinations they passed, of an outward show of clothes more European than those worn by the whites in tropical climates, and of timely excesses of polite posturing when they wished to impress. In comparison with these things, such petty manifestations of savage ingrained habits still prevalent as in their degenerate days of old, were not supposed to matter if they were discreetly shoved into the background for home use, and were not mentioned in white society.

THE GROWTH OF ETHIOPIANISM IN AFRICA

History has forgotten to hand down to us details concerning the actual taking over of African nationalism by the American negroes, nor did historians at the time take the trouble to discover the names of the principal leaders, who remained in the shade, took stock of the situation and reported it to headquarters across the Atlantic. They have not recorded facts which were then considered of so little consequence. Whereas somebody unknown, somebody very wide awake, realized at an early date that the discontented natives who could be reached through religious bodies of any sort were insufficient numerically to carry the movement forward. Also the unknown person recognized the fact that the majority of natives sturdily refused to let themselves be drawn out of their traditional sphere and that Africa was riddled with native secret societies of ancient lineage, on bad terms with the white invader on account of the sotadic rites and festivals they regaled themselves with. Further inquiry revealed a heartless persecution on the part of despotic white governments of all forms of indigenous entertainment, such as cannibalistic orgies and other home products, in consequence of which the members of the said societies repaid the white man with the strongest aversion.

History here is again at fault, for it is also not known how contact was established between two such antagonistic groups as the pagan and the native religious societies, hitherto separated by a gulf of antipathy and hatred that seemed too great to be surmounted. Nevertheless it is definitely ascertained that, by an unknown and unsuspected agency, liaison between them had by 1903 been established, and collaboration in the seductive game of white-man-baiting and white-man-fighting had been secured. Possibly it might not be going too far to specify that the rôle of baiting was assigned to the Ethiopians and that of fighting to the pagan secret societies. These will be gone into later; for the moment it is more expedient to continue with African xenophobia under the garb of Ethiopianism.

* * * * *

When Ethiopianism collapsed like a pricked balloon somewhere between 1898 and 1899, white sceptics in Africa hugged themselves in effusive congratulation, snapping derisive fingers and sneering insolently at the alarmists. Their complacency was rudely shaken when the first riots broke out in the Transkei in 1902 and they discovered them to have been negotiated by American negro ministers, thereby giving proof of the surreptitious return of the Watchtower to Africa. Those riots were soon quelled after some bloodshed, but others broke out soon afterwards and never since then has there been peace for long in the land. Riots and rebellions have broken out in frequent and continuous succession in different and far-distant regions, each time growing in intensity and marking a serious improvement in organization, and it is not possible to enumerate them. Some details about the more interesting Ethiopian rebellions will be given to illustrate the methods adopted to induce the natives to rise. The preliminaries of an outbreak are always the same. An agent arrives at some native centre and settles down unobtrusively, getting immediately into touch with the malcontents and the ambitious. He sympathizes exaggeratedly with them for their woes and the injuries inflicted upon them by white rule, making mountains out of molehills, twisting measures taken in the interests of the natives, such as cattle-dipping, into arguments for instilling animosity and the hope of rebellion. Their accomplishment in this field is amazing and bewildering, for no detail is too insignificant to escape their notice, facts are manipulated so as to give verisimilitude to the most astonishing and incongruous events, that are aptly and variously explained to suit the mentality of the audience or the exigencies of the moment, and to foster not only present irritation but apprehension for the future. It is on the chances of leadership that revolt depends, for unless a leader arises their discontent remains sterile.

The impulse of leadership descends suddenly

and unaccountably on a man, but his fate infallibly depends on the amount of mystery with which he can envelop his pretensions to having been invested with a supernatural wisdom from above, conferred on him in special circumstances. This gives an unquestionable prestige and authority, and the person thus favoured is able to impose his will on his more unsophisticated comrades. However, it must be borne in mind that many natives are acutely neurotic, even downright epileptic, so that it is hardly surprising that when such creatures are subjected to the atmosphere of religious exaltation, as is frequently the case with mission boys, they should really see themselves in visions and in dreams as the predestined liberators of the black race, when the sincerity of the urge for a messianic life must be conceded to them.

Nor is it necessary that the dream or vision should come directly to a man, for it has sometimes been known to have come to other people. Of course once the idea of leadership is suggested to him, he immediately follows it up as best he can. In some instances when a man understands that a golden opportunity is presented and that the ground is favourable for setting out on the road of rebellion, he just fakes up a trumpery vision or dream, and trusts to his luck to prove it.

Ecphonesis and oneiromancy are the mainstays of leadership, for the indecipherable cry of an epileptic, or a dream clear enough in its meaning to be understood by everybody, or through the interpretation of a witch-doctor, is sufficient to establish the repute of a leader, and push a tribe to revolt. Only those who have lived in understanding and familiarity with natives can appreciate the importance of dreams in primitive society, as for them a dream is the direct contact with their unknown tribal spirit N'Kos, who chooses this way of conveying his wishes to his people, besides being the recognized medium of communication with their departed ancestors who all resort to this method of warning, advising or admonishing their descendants. Many missionaries and civil servants who cannot succeed in winning the confidence of the tribe they are working among, marvel at a sudden change in the attitude of the natives, and fail to grasp the reason why their predecessors obtained a better hearing; or maybe were met with an unexpected friendship on arrival that dissolved unaccountably one day. These sudden veerings are constantly due to some dream.

Unfortunately the restrictions of the colour bar and other limitations render it practically impossible for an African to satisfy his craving to get into the limelight except by joining some revolutionary body, and the one career of never-failing satisfaction open to any native in any part of South and Central Africa today is that of seditionist. He is immediately hailed as a beacon of

THE SEETHING AFRICAN POT

light, collects a following of thousands, emerges from drab obscurity to a position of eminence and prestige, wins control of money and a wider opportunity for indulging surreptitiously in vice and of gratifying his more unregenerate impulses. The seditionist party attracts men and women of indisputable cleverness, ability and courage, though so far the women have only distinguished themselves as apostles, ready to participate in riots and rebellions, often as much to the fore as men, but only as lieutenants and not as generals. The indispensable ally of the leader is the witch-doctor, without whose support his power evaporates, for the assumption that the Bantu tribes hurl themselves into battle in complete disregard of death is entirely false; they unfailingly seek the services of the witch-doctor as a necessary precaution preceding any act in life. His mission varies in detail according to the district and the matter in hand, but the principles are the same.

The pagan and Christianized natives of South and Central Africa do not enter into combat with any idea of sacrificing their lives for a cause, but rather in perfect confidence that the powers of witchcraft will deliver them from peril. Without the witch-doctor not one of them would dare expose himself in combat. It is the witch-doctor who, by throwing his bones, invoking the tribal spirits and observing all omens, guarantees the pretentions to leadership of the claimant, sanc-

THE GROWTH OF ETHIOPIANISM IN AFRICA

tions the rebellion, pronounces on the choice of moment for it, and finally dispenses medicines and charms to preserve all concerned against the dangers of the enterprise. He must provide that steel shall not cut or pierce, and that bullets shall be deflected or miraculously transformed at the instant of touching the body of the anointed. Invisibility in time of danger and safety from detection for the rebels are invariably part of his stock-in-trade.

* * * * *

Central Africa may boast of being well to the fore in politico-religious infatuation, as the natives of those regions distinguished themselves considerably by their various insurrections. Loyal admirers and docile pupils of the Watchtower abound there, and the first-fruits of Ethiopianism ripened as early as 1902. Then the riots of Bailundu, and in 1907 the more important ones of Ambriz-Ambrizette put Angola into a state of confusion. The Elijah rebellion in Nigeria and the Malaki one in Uganda proved to headquarters in America that their delegates in Africa were worthy of their hire.

In Nyasaland, the native acolyte, John Chilembwe, considered that the moment when white men were engaged in war was propitious for a rising. In 1915 he abandoned his mission and started the usual native dissident church where he secretly delivered seditious sermons and fomented revolt. There do not seem to be any personal descriptions of the man, but that he was of the most primeval type there can be little doubt, for he thought that by murdering the few whites unabsorbed by the War the land would be rid of the dominant race for evermore. That he was exceedingly crafty there is equally no doubt, for, after fixing a day long ahead for the execution of his plan, he went about from tribe to tribe enlisting dissatisfied native chiefs in the cause, without raising the suspicion of the whites. Actually not a whisper of the unrest reached the whites, and on the appointed day a column of rebels assembled at the meeting-place indicated by Chilembwe. Under his personal guidance they successively surrounded three outlying white farms, murdered the whites they found in them, and marched on Mandale.

By an extremely strange coincidence the settlers had that day held in the town a meeting that was just breaking up, and they were getting into their cars to go home when the rebels arrived within hearing distance. Motor-cars in those days normally emitted a series of bangs before starting, and this concerto of explosions given simultaneously by a number of cars was mistaken for machine-gun fire by the natives who, thinking themselves discovered, fled in such confusion as to betray their presence to the unsuspecting whites. After rushing their women and children to safety into

THE GROWTH OF ETHIOPIANISM IN AFRICA

an improvised place of refuge, the settlers started to form a band to fight the rebels. Luckily Chilembwe was so disconcerted at having the tables turned on him that he rather lost his head, giving the whites time to collect their forces, for the situation might have become extremely grave if the rebels had had a proper leader and pressed their advantage.

Given the opportunity to make their preparations the whites quickly organized an offensive that overcame the rebels at the first attack, definitely dispersing them. Chilembwe succeeded in escaping during the fight, but was chased and killed just when near the border of the Portuguese territory in which he had counted on losing himself.

But the movement assumed really vast proportions and became a menace when the Congolese epileptic catechist, Simon Kibangu, received the messianic call. He had suffered from fits and convulsions since early boyhood, and probably his whole nature was affected by the mystical atmosphere of the mission. One day, as is the nature of his kind, he had a vision in which he saw himself as the Black Saviour of the Black Race, while an unearthly voice bade him gird up his loins and depart on his errand. Firmly believing himself to be inspired by God to free his downtrodden race, he promptly shook the dust of the mission from his willing feet and launched a violent anti-white campaign on the very scene of his past labours.

Returning to his home at Nkamba, Kibangu staged miracles to consolidate his reputation, and from every quarter natives trooped over the paths to see him, bringing him their dead to raise and their sick to heal, and to listen to his wonderful preaching and prophesies. Hence arose the title of Prophet which was conferred on him by his sect, and assumed by him officially, thereby introducing a new fashion which was eagerly adopted among religious agitators of the region, who up to that time had been called Ethiopians. But it must be borne in mind that Black Prophetism is another manifestation of Ethiopianism, and in essence the same thing. In cases however where the utterances of the Prophets have given the direct stimulus to revolt, the Prophets themselves, though remaining spiritual leaders and advisers, do not necessarily head the rebellion in person.

Kibangu used his Bible aptly to represent himself to his fellow people in a way to impress them. He made his appearance after a long interval surrounded by a band of exulting followers, taking away the breath of his audience by his long flowing robes of shining silk, advancing with slow gait and rapturous expression, raising his arms in theatrical benediction or laying his hands on the sick with pontifical solemnity. And then the awed silence of the palpitating crowd would be broken by his voice thrilling their souls with his magical discourses. One day he was David overthrowing the giant Goliath; on another, he was Judas Maccabeus championing the oppressed Congolese, or Moses leading the Israelites out of the desert into the land of Canaan, all meant as parables to be applied to the black and white races.

The authorities of the colony had been warned of Kibangu's sect, but no notice was taken of it for a long time, not till the cries and groans of his congregation had changed their significance, and the forests had been made to ring with, "Down with the oppressor! Down with enforced labour and taxes! Down with Bula Matari!" [1]

The agitation developed unchecked, growing more and more into sheer fanaticism. By Kibangu's order the fields were left unsown, on the promise of possession of the fields of the white men in the very near future. Personal passes and tax receipts were destroyed as a defiance. Soon Kibangu had his own apostolic college; new prophets arose like mushrooms in one night, many women being seized with the inspiration to go forth as crusaders in Kibangu's name. The plan was made to attack the plantations of Kitobola and appropriate the great rice deposits to feed the men. They succeeded in secretly opening a route in the north bank of the Congo River, be-

[1] Native expression for Belgian rule.

tween Boko and Brazzaville, before the authorities were alive to the danger of what was preparing, and the territorial chief was ordered to make an inquiry.

Troops were sent out from Boma to Thysville with the order to arrest Kibangu. They surrounded the village of Nkamba, but Kibangu himself slipped through their fingers and was not arrested until long afterwards. He was sent as a prisoner to Thysville, but his passage through the city was the triumphal progress of a Messiah, and but for the determined attitude of the authorities the excitement might easily have turned to revolt. Kibangu was condemned to death, but the missionaries intervened on his behalf, and he was deported to Elisabethville for life. Kibangism, however, has never wholly subsided, and recrudescences occur from time to time. In 1924 there was another outbreak in the Tumba district. Six thousand natives collected in the environs of Thysville, claiming the liberation of the prisoner and the right to pray according to their own rites. They could not be dispersed for four days. As recently as November 1929 similar incidents which occurred at Bandakami and Thysville have called people's attention to the fact that the Kibangu sedition was not yet exhausted. In 1931 agitation became so widespread that energetic measures had to be taken, after which the Congo Press openly commented on the narrow escape from a serious Kibangu general rising. From the Belgian Congo the agitation soon passed into Angola, infecting the natives there with a great unrest. Very soon after this the Congolese catechist, Pedro Goluvo, had, or gave out that he had had, a vision, and announced himself as the prophet for Angola. His example was soon followed by Paul Bokele, Pedro Makasi, Pedro Swana, Pedro Tamlica and Alvaro Nzaki, all of whom assumed the title of prophet. Prophetism in Angola followed pretty much on the lines set by Kibangu. Fields were to be cultivated only for as much as was required for native consumption, with the object of chasing the whites away by famine. Personal passes and tax receipts were again destroyed. This advice was closely followed at least at S. Salvador where food became scarce. When rioting broke out in 1927 the Portuguese authorities intervened energetically, but not till the next year was order restored. The leader Pedro Goluvo escaped to his native land and managed to disappear, but the others were cast into prison.

III SECRET SOCIETIES OF CENTRAL AFRICA

The question why all Africans are so devoted to secret societies, some of which indulge in terrifying practices loathed by those natives who do not belong to them, in a land where squeamishness is absent, has often been asked and never satisfactorily answered. Centuries of such traditions have left their indelible mark on the negro mind, as is proved by those in America who, after three hundred years' absence from Africa, still indulge in as many kindred organizations as they can manage. They have set up in the alien land innumerable burial, benefit and secret societies to which every man, woman and child belongs as their time and means allow.

It is evident that from its earliest days the African child is trained to aspire to membership of some secret association, at least a "school" or "lodge" for the initiation into manhood or womanhood. The ceremonies are invariably attended with great secrecy, and even accidental and involuntary revelation of its mysteries is punished with barbarous severity. Possibly this used to be imposed with such stringency to give the drilling in secretiveness which was indispensable for tribal and individual safety at a period when these might depend on the stoical suppression of evidence at the cost of any personal suffering, by prisoners made in war or seized by raiders.

The physical operations to which the youth of both sexes are subjected open up many other sides to the question. They are part of the training to stoicism through physical pain to which all members of the tribe must be inured in a land where torture was systematically used by an enemy to extort information which might jeopardize the safety of the community. Because undoubtedly no effort to minimize pain was or is made, and the cruel abuse of corporal punishment demands an explanation.

On the other hand there is also the ritualistic aspect, which may be seen in the ceremonial presentation to the spirits of the departed ancestors of their young descendants at the moment of emerging from childhood to take their place in the family and kraal, to obtain their protection against danger.

It is further the great coming-of-age festival which marks the passage from childhood to manhood and womanhood, after which the participant can marry, and for the boys it represents also the call to arms, the conscription as a warrior with all its dignity and duties, honours and perils.

In those tribes (they are not all) where such operations are customary, the man or the woman who has not undergone them will have great difficulty in finding a mate, for they constitute the preparation, physical and moral, for parenthood. The man would be considered unclean and the woman be branded as hopelessly barren, even in cases where ocular proof to the contrary is forthcoming; for the fear of having incurred the displeasure of the spirits of the ancestors and of having to bear the consequences of breaking tribal law, is regarded as bound to result in weak offspring, and would prevent the parents and clan of the intending couple from consenting to the union. Besides these religious scruples, for the men they were a warranty of full virility as warriors and tribesmen, and riveted the fealty to their chief. In many tribes the "school" is only held for the boys when there is the son of the chief ready to enter it, for the boys of his class will thereafter constitute his party, his councillors and bodyguard, stand with him through life, and sometimes go with him if he is driven into exile. It is further an avowal on their part of belonging to the tribe, and on the part of the tribe an acknowledgment that it recognizes them as fully fledged and responsible members of it. So much so that a man belonging to one tribe, who years before had satisfied all the demands of his tribal creed, on removing to another part of the land

and wishing to be admitted to citizenship among his new neighbours, if it is a tribe where the same customs prevail, is often obliged to undergo a second initiation in company with some of its members for naturalization.

Missionaries have tried from the first to stop these coming-of-age lodges on the ground of the licentiousness and immorality unfortunately attending them, and of the undoubted brutality of the operations performed on the girls, for which everybody maintains there is no necessity at all. As usual they have defeated their own ends by handling the situation too drastically and trenchantly, by imposing renunciation as a condition of baptism. Though there is a decided decrease in the intensity of the practice, the apparent acquiescence on the part of the natives produces the unedifying spectacle of so-called Christian pupils of mission stations entering these "schools" and "lodges" belatedly, on the completion of the missionary course, having necessarily deferred the ceremonies till the moment when the cloak of Christianity could be conveniently dropped and they could resume their freedom to revel wholeheartedly in the forbidden festivities.

In some valleys there is the other phenomenon of tribes which, after about eighty years' abolition, have revived these practices in what amounts to a wave of collective revulsion against the restrictions of Christianity.

THE SEETHING AFRICAN POT

Real progress on the other hand has been made where the missionaries concede circumcision to the boys on condition that it is performed in a hospital, and that the operations on the girls are reduced to a symbolic execution of them, countenancing at the same time the more innocent festivities.

Nor is it possible to dismiss the problem without taking into consideration the social side of it, the human propensity for amusement and excitement to break the monotony of life, and the world-wide need for rejoicing and banqueting. All races celebrate in some way the coming of age of their offspring, and few opportunities are neglected to exchange hospitality with friends on established occasions in life.

In primitive life there are certain religious festivals and family celebrations to be observed, which would be extremely difficult to replace until a new tribal organization is reached. Christians would be wise to remember that as long as the fifth century after the death of the Saviour, the popular festivities for Venus had not been overcome. And it was only by substituting the Nativity that they were transformed at all. The population that for a thousand years had celebrated one of the hugest festivals in its calendar on December the 25th, could only be induced to forget Venus by having another religious figure put in her place.

To return to the natives of Africa. Missionary field work again shows the tragic consequences of lack of insight by irrationally attempting to suppress all forms of amusement on the incontestable grounds of immorality. It forbade the initiation rites on grounds of turpitude, beer drinks as leading to drunkenness with its attendant evils of brawls and fights, native dances on the plea of their licentiousness, condemning the unfortunate natives to a demureness of behaviour quite foreign to their innate gaiety and sociability, forcing them to lead lives of an emptiness that would drive any normal human being frantic. Is it then surprising that the palpitating throb of drums summoning to a dance, or the passionate and blood-stirring songs of some pagan neighbours abandoning themselves to an orgy of feasting should prove an irresistible lure tempting them from their homes, forgetful of all hopes of glory everlasting in the next world in the immediate gratification of the delights of this one?

Besides, the increased demands of labour in the land and the pressure of taxation between them induce the vast majority of natives to visit towns at one time or other of their lives, where they not only learn how far the white man himself indulges in the pleasures of life, but they find provision for their own entertainment in the cinemas, dances and meetings, religious or seditious, that make a point of securing their favour. Further, in the exercise of their duties they taste the sweets of authority and the pride of promotion. On their return home can they be expected to be content without any form of excitement? Missionaries and the anti-white propaganda between them are equally responsible for the enormous growth of secret societies among the Bantu tribes, for while the aggravation of their virulence is due to the venom of propagandists, white and black, who make a profession of stirring up the natives against the white man, the excessive Christian puritanism of the missionaries, by depriving the natives of the means of enjoying themselves openly, has driven them, rather than renounce amusement, to find it surreptitiously by joining the secret societies for the celebration of sotadic festivals, to which they had not before been drawn.

One of the most noteworthy and fundamental characteristics of some of these secret societies is the adoption of a fetish, to which they attribute supernatural powers and offer sacrifices. This is particularly striking, as it is in complete contrast with the religious conceptions of the people among whom it flourishes, who are not idolatrous and have no idols in their normal religious worship.

CANNIBALISTIC SOCIETIES

The Anioto
(*Human Leopards and Human Crocodiles*)

So much has already been written about this secret society that another description of its customs would be superfluous. But a few less known additional details may be of interest.

In common with many others of its kind, it is an extremely ancient society, of immemorial origin. There is evidence that it has recently developed so extensively as to necessitate a reorganization of its constitution, and while a single supreme chief, who in 1933 was Bakwo, is still nominally recognized, the society has in effect split up into lodges for the convenience of initiation and other ceremonies.

The ruling spirit of the society is Borfimah, a contraction of Boreh-Fima, or medicine-bag, which is embodied in a fetish symbolically fashioned out of an oval gourd or leather pouch, filled with an unmentionable combination of filth. The principal ingredients are wax, clay and human blood and fat.

Initiation is a complicated affair about which much is still kept secret. However, it is established that cannibalistic orgies and offerings form one of its principal features, and even involuntary participation in these is said to constitute obligatory admission. Little is known of the principles on which the victim is selected, except that it must be fully grown, and may be of either sex. In some districts it must be a near relation of the novice. The flesh of the victim is literally torn slowly to shreds. The cruel knife used for this purpose may be seen at the British Museum.

THE SEETHING AFRICAN POT

As soon as death mercifully ends the torture, the internal organs are cut out of the body and examined by the presiding head of the lodge for augury. The kidneys and the skin of the forehead are said to be offered to Borfimah, which probably means that they are chopped up and mixed with the blood and fat. By the acceptance of the offering by the fetish, the body of the victim is believed to be sanctified by the spirit of Borfimah entering therein. Small pieces of the warm flesh are then eaten raw by all those present, and other small portions, wrapped separately in banana leaves, are despatched by special runners to the absent members of the lodge, who swallow them immediately on the supposition that they are still warm. The idea is almost that of a communion, as the real significance behind it is the common partaking of a sacrifice offered to Borfimah, who thereby enters into those who eat pieces of the body, to strengthen and protect them. This part of the initiation ceremony is supposed to be a recent importation and to be influenced by Christianity. Members of the society bear a distinguishing scar on their lips and bodies; this last they disclose to the victim they have chosen by pulling aside their loin-cloths. So dreaded is the society that it is rarely that anyone dares to offer any resistance when the messenger of torture and death suddenly presents himself. Nor do the friends and relations of the victim interfere to save him. The Leopards take a particular delight in presenting themselves at gatherings and carrying off their victim from amidst a crowd frozen and paralyzed with terror. To Borfimah are attributed such powers for good and evil that even non-members have faith in it. Christian natives known positively not to belong to the society have, when confronted and tested by the fetish, tremblingly admitted having perjured themselves on a sacred Bible oath, and have sobbed out some incriminating truth.

The Human Leopards flourish along the West Coast of Central Africa, and a few scattered lodges are found as far inland as the Belgian Congo. Along the rivers a variant of the society is found, as the members style themselves Crocodiles instead of Leopards, and disguise themselves in a framework representing a crocodile in order to perpetrate their crimes. This frame is known as the Koomkoo-Be, and some specimens have been seized by the Government of Sierra Leone. It is formed of two small canoes tightly fastened together, and the bow is an exact reproduction of a crocodile's head. Just below it there are two large holes for the member's hands. Through these he hauls his victim into the water with sharp iron claws as soon as he can reach him, and tears him to pieces. Sometimes they deliberately combine in a party and go beneath a canoe to upset it, proceeding then to drag their victims from the water. The Crocodiles, like the Leopards, worship the fetish Borfimah.

The Bakasandji and the Tupoyo

The Bakasandji is a secret cannibalistic society, membership of which is reserved exclusively to the witch-doctors, male or female. It assumes all its members to have enjoyed a miraculous resurrection, and initiation into the society consists mainly in passing through an apparent death. The headquarters of the society are at Kabengele, and the head priest is called the Bwana Mutombo. At one time he was the only person entitled to preside over the initiation ceremonies. But as the society throve and spread it became necessary to form branch communities under the administration of secondary heads empowered to admit postulants. The heads all acquire the title of Bwana Mutombo, and are addressed by their satellites as Tata, or father. Male members indulge in secret cannibalistic orgies in the depths of the forest, but these are forbidden to the female members who are allowed to feast only on the flesh of snakes. Their "medicine" or charm is called Bwanga Bwa Mpalu, and is kept in a horn called Nkishi. It serves to protect the initiates from the spirits of the bodies they feast upon, and from all other evil. This Bwanga Bwa Mpalu is composed of filthy substances, mixed with the crushed bones of the victims, human bones for the men and snake bones for the women. This is a rather notable feature, as it is quite unusual to find a charm differently concocted according to the sex of the user. After each feast the smaller bones of the victim are broken up and the charm refreshed with new offerings.

The simulated death already mentioned at the initiation ceremony is caused by an intoxicating beverage served hot to the novice that produces a kind of epileptic fit ending in unconsciousness. The beverage is made out of the fruit of the Lupajipaji plant which is cultivated expressly for the use of the witch-doctors in the exercise of their numerous duties. Its first effects are a foaming at the mouth, then comes a trembling which ends in the fit proper. As soon as the potion is drunk the novice is bidden to dance, and is supposed to dance until he drops down in such complete insensibility that the onlookers may test it by pinching, pricking, stamping on the prostrate body and various other amiabilities. On recovering his senses the novice is told that death had taken him, and that he has been recalled to life by Bwana Bwa Mpalu who has now taken possession of his body and will protect him from all evil if he observes the cult. As it may take a strong man anything up to three days, it is affirmed, before becoming insensible, and a complete unconsciousness cannot be relied on for certain, offerings are judiciously made to the proper quarter to allow him to drop after a few hours of dancing and simulate unconsciousness. These privileges however vary in cost according to the condition of the initiate. After consciousness has been restored, the postulant is given a piece of smoked human flesh to eat, and another potion to drink that contains the powdered forehead bone of the skull of a near relation, such as one of his parents or an elder brother. The remainder of the skull is placed solemnly in his hands by the Bwana Mutombo, who bids him keep it ever at his head when he lies down to sleep, as it will preserve him from danger and sickness, and aid him in any venture. Sometimes the ordinary course of events in a wild life provides a suitable skull for the ceremony; failing that the novice must attend to the matter as discreetly as he can. These ceremonies over, the elected can whitewash his face and don his regalia, the Nkaka. He is given a little time to produce a body for the feast in the forest to celebrate his nomination. Apparently murder is rarely done to procure one, as a freshly-buried corpse may generally be exhumed for the repast. The member must however wear his full regalia during the process for it to be ritualistically valid. Women have an easier initiation ceremony.

    The Bakasandji society is probably the most

ancient one in the district, and the parent stock of all the other minor societies that flourish there. The Tupoyo society is very like it and is probably as old. It is however really a moot point which of the two was the first to start, especially as they prosper in the same area.

Desertion from the ranks of both entails trial by the society and sentence of death, which, though passed on the culprit, is rarely carried out. As a rule they content themselves with kidnapping the offender and carrying him off to the forest for a mild torture. But on the day of his death, however distant, they will devour his body like that of an outsider instead of respecting it like that of a fellow-member.

The Tupoyo has practically the same organization as the Bakasandji, with the exception that its women members are allowed to partake of the banquets of human flesh with the men instead of being restricted to separate feasts of snake's meat. There are also some minor differences, but initiation and exhumation in full regalia are the same for the men of both societies.

Very important, however, are the bad relations between them and the Bakasandji; there is always ill will between the two societies that may very easily end in bloody frays. Apparently they respect each other's corpses.

There seem to be quite a number of minor secret societies with endless ramifications branching through the land, crowded together and overlapping each other, supposed to be offshoots of one of these two larger ones. The Bayembe and Bene Nkole of the Lujima Watershed, and the Kitwimina, may be instanced among many. Wherever any of these sects are to be found, no person may be sure of securing a safe burial for his body. It is a very common practice for those who dislike the idea of disinterment and of providing meat for the sabba, to come to terms with the ruling society of his district so as to avert desecration of his grave after death. But in a great many cases, although large sums have been paid and gifts given, if the new corpse is in the least toothsome the grave is violated, and any protests by relations are met with preposterous excuses and threats. The really revolting part of the business lies in the fact that many respected natives, of a superior education and occupying important posts under white administration, natives reputed to be civilized and progressive, still belong to these societies.

The only good point about them is their common hate for the Bumbudye. Whenever they come across this society they bury their differences and join forces to attack it, and they always end by destroying the lodge and cleaning the place of its presence; declaring that natives once impressed into it are shorn hopelessly of their natural decency by such degrading customs!

SECRET SOCIETIES OF CENTRAL AFRICA

NON-CANNIBALISTIC SOCIETIES

The Balwaba or Bumbudye

The sect calls itself the Balwaba from Kwabe, to share, as its members are supposed to, and do, share with each other their worldly goods, down to their food and women. They are called the Bumbudye by outsiders, who in their turn are called the Bangulungu by the Bumbudye.

The sect professes to be a society of dancers, and it counts some extremely clever ones among its members, and gives public exhibitions deserving the highest praise; however, the dancing is nothing but a mask to hide the real object of the society, which is sexual excess, feasting and living richly at the expense of the Bangulungu, or on the proceeds of the vicious circle of fines, imposed on outsiders and even on the members for the slightest slip in the observance of their infinitely complicated system of signs, countersigns, passwords and ritual. All tradition as to the derivation and original meaning of the sect is completely lost. It may at one time have been one of the weird religions to be found in Africa, and possibly the ritual may have had symbolic meanings now totally forgotten. There is also a special language of about 200 words that its members must use among themselves. This language does not resemble the one spoken in Lubaland or surrounding districts, but may be a survival, handed down from generation to generation, from forgotten ancestors living in some far region of Africa.

The Balwaba sect has some special features differentiating it from similar ones, chiefly its mixed membership, which offers the unique example of a membership of men, women and children; its methods for violently compelling individuals to join by means of fines, persecution and torture, when persuasion fails, its lack of a supreme chief or general headquarters. Every tribal chieftainship or district has a lodge, called the Kinyengele, where the members collect in session. Each Kinyengele has its own set of officials, but the calls and signals are the same for all the lodges.

The headman is called the Kikungulu by the sect, and Tshikala by the Bangulungu. He is appointed by the chief of the district or by someone of the same degree in other lodges, in the case of a new Kinyengele being set up. He is the President and dominates all other officials, and has a subordinate under him, a sort of secretary, called the Ndalamba, to help carry out his orders.

The second in command is the Musenge, who apportions the work to the members. The Tusulu is the steward to whom gifts and fines are handed. The Lwaba is an underling of his for dispensing the gifts and food, while the drink is given into the care of the Mfum'wa Seya, who is always a woman, in contrast to the native custom. These distributors of food and drink are distinguishable by a tuft of feathers worn on the side of the head. The Mfum'Bana is the guardian of the child-members, and acts *in loco parentis*.

The Bwana Mukanba wa Kilo is the chief engineer and has to build the Kinyengele. He has the right to exact an indemnity for his labour, in the form of a toll, from every member including those who partake in the work of erection. The lodge is always set up in the secret recesses of the forest with one path leading up to it, guarded by a triple row of five gates each, frequently provided with man pits and traps.

The Kaloba is responsible for clearing the path and keeping the grounds clean. He has the right to identify them with his own person and to regard any soiling of them as a personal insult, for which he may claim indemnity. The Mashinda is in charge of the path leading to the Kinyengele, and receives tribute from everybody who uses it, although this is compulsory to reach the gates. The actual porter who, on the password only, admits people to the lodge is the Kibelo. Then there is the lodge's policeman, the Minkwanza, who always, even when dancing, wears a rope coiled round his shoulders, with which to bind offenders. The Kamandji is the master of the ceremonies who gives the signal for the dancing to begin or to stop, decides what figures shall be danced, orders the change of step, and commands silence. The Mukabo, instead, is the master of the death ceremonies; he prescribes the rites to lay the ghost of the departed, and the funeral dances and beer-drinks.

These are only the principal offices. With the exception of the Mfum'wa Seya, who must always be a woman, they are held generally by men, and only occasionally by a woman. There is further a complicated set of degrees of membership, of which the highest is that of the stoat, which confers on the holder the right to sleep on the skin of this animal.

The Bumbudye deity is a fabulous female animal supposed to be the offspring of a woman and a buffalo. She is called Lolo Inamombe, familiarly contracted to Lo Nombe, or Lolo or Nombe alone, and is represented as a buffalo with a woman's head and breasts. Most incongruously, the living embodiment of this deity is the land tortoise, the Kichidi, which being a delicacy in Lubaland, is much sought after by the Bangulungu. Indeed, a favourite test of a native's feelings towards the society is to introduce a kichidi into his premises and watch his behaviour. If he is kind to it, he is understood to be well disposed towards the sect; if he ill-treats it or shows signs of preparing to kill it, the animal is bought off by a member. A Shambudye calls it his mother and really reverences it, and woe betide the imprudent person who tries to hurt one. Sometimes a kichidi may be in the hands of someone not to be scared by the sect, in which case a truly high ransom may be offered for its release.

The lodges are independent and as a rule get on well with each other, yet quarrels do occasionally break out, and are followed by fights that strew the ground with dead and wounded. Sometimes one lodge acquires a temporary supremacy over neighbouring ones, but that is due to personal prestige of the board. During the sessions at the Kinyengele there are dances and beer-drinks which all members must attend, women alone being exempted for reasons that are strictly verified. Each man can generally choose the woman he wants, only the Kikungulu having the right to two. The woman has no option, and must submit to any man, even if it be her father, brother or son; however, incest is rare. Adultery outside the sect is forbidden to the member, promiscuity among the members not counting as such.

When the Kinyengele is in session every Shambudye (member) claims the privilege of deference from the Bangulungu. Bangulungu are forbidden to remain on the path when meeting a member, and they must get off it, bow humbly, and pour dust on their heads in sign of inferiority. Nor may an outsider remain seated, even if it be under the verandah of his own house, nor stand in the shade within sight of a passing Shambudye. Fines and torture are the penalty, for the sect maintains the strictest solidarity and an insult offered to any member is an insult to the whole body. It boasts of its vengeance from which it claims that no one ever escapes. Nor does pre-existing friendship or relationship bring exemption from observation of these rules; and new members not wearing regalia and initiated so recently that the fact is unknown are equally entitled to receive homage. In case a member fails to denounce any omission that can be proved against him, fines and torture are applied to him as well as to the offender. Fines may be in money or in kind; torture is of various kinds and applied with ruthless and refined cruelty.

In the first stages the culprits may be bound and kept out in the sun all day, a thing not even natives can stand. Or the sufferers may be bound to the roof of a thatched hut where the smoke emerging from a smouldering fire inside chokes them. Or they may be bound to a tree and hot cinders pressed between their toes. Or the famous mulongo torture may be inflicted, consisting in rolling and tying the victim in the stiff midribs of the large palms, with head and feet sticking out of the bundle. The helpless body is lifted from the ground and dropped from an ever-increasing height. Those who have experienced it declare that the concussion on the hard ground

SECRET SOCIETIES OF CENTRAL AFRICA

even from the height of a few inches, when there is nothing to soften the impact and the body is forcibly rigid, gives a frightful jar that takes the breath away, and when repeated easily conduces to crippling the victim for life or to killing him. In some exceptional cases obdurate subjects have had their wrappings set alight, their executioners standing by to put out the flames when the suitable moment seems to them to have arrived. If their judgment is wrong the victim may be dead or dying when released. One does not hear of deliberate death-sentences being passed, but those in charge very lightly and insouciantly push punishment to the extremes of suffering, careless of maiming and causing the death of the offender. Many crippled natives cannot be induced to reveal the cause of their misfortune, for the Bambudye terrorize the whole land, and no individual can resist them or be safe from their cruel vengeance. The tribal chiefs themselves are helpless and there are many instances of quite important ones being kidnapped and taken to the forest to be released only on the terms of their captors, usually membership, or at least toleration, of the lodge on their land. On the other hand as the Kikungulu pays the chief of the district 100 francs tribute every time the sect assembles in the Kinyengele, and each dancer also pays a heavy toll to him for the right to dance, it is highly improbable that fear is the decisive factor in their toleration, but rather that they prefer not to dry up the source of an abundant income by excessive prudery.

A very special procedure, sometimes evidently artfully studied to be in direct contradiction with the prevailing customs of the country, marks the behaviour of the Balwaba. This is adopted probably with the intention of making the detection of an intruder inevitable, and to provide occasion for fining inattentive members, as any omission is severely and inexorably dealt with. Both of food and of drink a little must be left over, and when a mat is given to sit on, it is spread out in the place allotted; a corner of it is then turned up, and the Shambudye sits on the ground beneath it. The Kinyengele may only be entered by the eastern door and left by the western one. None of the sect rises to greet the tribal chief on any occasion while the lodge is in session, and it may be that the tribute of 100 francs is paid to obtain this exemption. Much banqueting on the animals extorted in fines goes on, and much drinking. An offering of beer must be sent to the chief; but the bearers keep at a distance from his house and put it down on the ground, remaining to sing him a couple of songs. Voluntary membership undoubtedly is common owing to the variety of the entertainments.

The session ended, each member returns home, but gatherings are continually held to try offenders, to apply punishment, to attend the lengthy initiation rites and for various other amusing reasons. Besides which, visits between lodges are exchanged, and sometimes three or four join together in a sort of jamboree. On their way any attractive women or proud possessors of flourishing stock that they meet, any offenders against the enforced code of respect demanded by the Bambudye, are all pressed into membership by fair means of persuasion or by the foul extortion of fines and torture. Obstinate resistance leads to the poisoning of individuals and sometimes to the wiping out of whole families. Given the circumstances and the environment, recalcitrant people rarely dare to maintain their resistance to the end.

Initiation for a man is very intricate and lasts over a long time. The process begins by the offering of a cock and a hen, two rows of small beads and two of larger ones. Then the candidate is led blindfold by his two sponsors, one representing a lion and the other a leopard, into all sorts of traps and into water to test his courage. He is cut on the chest to draw blood, and made to eat a still warm fowl's liver that symbolizes his own. At the end of the first tests the novice may smear his face with ash.

In the second stage he is bidden greet a little wooden image, Kipukapuka, the meaning of which is unknown, then to strike it with his

THE SEETHING AFRICAN POT

knuckles till he has skinned them. Then the figure is pulled by a concealed cord and made to duck as a signal that Lolo Inamombe will graciously accept the novice, but he is told that he must dance till she gives another signal that she is ready to receive him. So he dances till he is informed that Lolo is ready, when he is conducted to a covered pit, into which he is told to put his hand to receive Lolo's gift, usually a few white beads in token of her pleasure at acquiring a new devotee. The novice is complimented by his sponsors and the members crowd round him. He is then invited to try his luck a second time, which he invariably does. But this time one of his fingers is caught between the strong teeth of a man concealed in the pit, and the torture begins. He is told to confess all his past indiscretions, all his failings, all the most unsavoury details of his life, and is forced to admit any accusations made by the Balwaba surrounding him. When they have finished extorting from him a full confession, and they realize there is nothing more he can confess or be brought to admit, they ask him what he will give to be released, and a regular bargaining ensues. Twenty francs, fifty francs, as much as represents the man's utmost limit. Not till then does he recover his mangled finger, accompanied by the warning that if he has omitted any interesting revelation Lolo will be aware of it and kill him. This public disclosure prevents resipiscence and recantation and the chance of quitting the society. He is then admonished that revelation of any kind of the doings of the society is forbidden on pain of fine or torture, that it is equally iniquitous for the Bangulungu to ask him questions, and that any question or mark of disrespect must be reported. He then again smears his nose with ash and the second part of the initiation is complete. He has reached the stage of Mbudye Mwana.

The final initiation ceremony, the Kusubula, does not take place till some time later when the Mbudye Mwana has had time to learn the signals, calls, signs, countersigns, secret language and rules of behaviour belonging to the sect, and is ready to pay the final fees. At the end of the third test he is a full-fledged Shambudye, may smear his face with white chalk, wear the regalia and partake in the ceremonies and entertainments of the society.

Initiation, in special circumstances, can be done under the direction of any member, but it is usually conducted under that of the Tusulu, who has a special regalia for the occasion.

The initiation of women is scarcely a ceremony at all; that of children is done by the Mfum'Bana, who sits on the ground and arches a leg, under the knee of which the novice has to crawl twice. The first time he or she must crawl under it without touching it, crawl round its guardian and pass again. As the novice's head appears from under the bended knee the Mfum'Bana seizes it by the hair and bangs it smartly on the ground. Then the child stands up and knocks its head hard, forehead against forehead, against the guardian's. If on either occasion it shows signs of pain, it is severely punished.

Any stranger straying into their midst, or following the path to the Kinyengele in perfect innocence, is never stopped, but once well in is seized and is lucky to escape with his life after paying heavy fines or suffering torture.

Bangulungu, who give the lodge presents of beer and animals, are invited to the Kinyengele to partake of the feast and entertainment, and afterwards are allowed to choose a woman. The society extends over an area about four hundred miles long and nearly as wide.

* * * * *

The aforementioned societies all date back from time immemorial, and probably still celebrate ancient rites handed down from generation to generation, the significance of which they have completely lost, together with any recollection of the country of their origin. Students of African ritualistic sects rather incline to believe that they may at one time have been religious cults involving human sacrifice and ending in banquets on those parts of the victim not required for the religious ceremony. They think that through the centuries the religious part of the creed may have fallen into disuse, the human victimization for the purpose of cannibalistic feasts alone surviving in a land of general cannibalism. In this way the natives can surreptitiously indulge savage impulses and feed their carnal and bloodthirsty lusts. They can satisfy their intuitive passion for orgies, their craving for the exercise of power and for the gratification of inspiring terror in outsiders by a form of moral outlawry from tribal restraint and tradition.

This theory seems especially appropriate in the case of the Bambudye, whose whole system of secret code in words, signs, countersigns, and behaviour, contrasts in every detail with the manners of the country where they have been living for the last few centuries. It may possibly at one time have been the only means of recognizing members of the tribe unknown personally in an alien land, or may be equally the survival of the forgotten language and customs of their original country maintained among themselves as a ritual, much as the present-day emigrants and exiles keep up in the privacy of the family gatherings the language and the celebrations of the native countries for which they are homesick.

However, even if this is the correct interpretation of the ancient societies, it does not explain the constitution of the Ntambwe Bwanga secret society which made an unobtrusive entry into the Belgian Congo probably about 1920. It was first noted in 1922, and rapidly overran the land, extending into Angola. It is a cancerous growth of racial hatred deliberately cultivated on modern lines by a master mind well versed in native lore, with a profound knowledge of how to make the complicated appeal to native psychology, of how to blend subtly the native's primitive aspiration to belong to a secret society, feed his animal appetites, and gratify his ambition to ape the white man. The society provides him with the means of gratifying the former to the accompaniment of terrible rites already existing in the land, and enables him at the same time cleverly to pander to his worst respectabilities.

This weird association was conceived with the hope of canalizing prevalent wasted forces and of uniting likely subversive elements into a homogeneous body, regularly subdivided into a complete organization under carefully chosen leaders. These were deputed to guide the undirected impulses and break in the undisciplined natives to teamwork, through the observance of clearly defined rules, and obedience to clearly defined orders, so that they should be ready for use when eventually needed. The master mind who planned out the Ntambwe Bwanga society remains for the present modestly in the background. Some day perhaps he may reveal himself, and claim the praise which is his due for so magisterially conjuring with such uncompromisingly barbarous material. With an amazing insight into the psychology and tastes of the natives, he has played upon their inherent weaknesses in such a way as to appeal infallibly to all their fundamental frailties and feelings. He has turned the resources of the native tribes into a danger whose potentiality is the more alarming that it is hidden, and reveals itself so far only in its terrorism.

There is no doubt that by 1922 the Belgian Congo was thickly honeycombed with different exponents of anti-white propaganda in all the districts where natives lived; but the Katanga climate is unfavourable to the negro, and the district was very sparsely inhabited until the white man arrived to open mines, build towns, lay down railways, etc. The economic labour opportunities caused thousands of natives to flock there from all parts of the country. They met without past friendships to bind them together or past feuds to enliven the deadly monotony of the leisure hours. Christian natives found white missionaries or native dissident churches ready to receive them with open arms, to comfort and entertain them with services and meetings; but the raw natives, the pagans, roamed about at a loose end like lost souls, missing their secret societies, longing for an outlet for the sordes in their nature and a chance to practise the many nefarious customs they had indulged in while living at home. Pan-

THE SEETHING AFRICAN POT

African propaganda was actively stirring up sinister clamourings and holding out vague promises of the speedy removal of an oppression to be endured for but little longer. It was fanning the sullen disaffection which had become by now the ordinary mood and natural temper of the land. It was systematically harping on the artificially created hankering to get back to primitive conditions of barbarity, representing it as the natural growth of their own manhood and tradition, but any actual organization fusing the disbanded elements of distant secret societies was lacking. A report warned the revolutionary headquarters and a careful study was made of how to remedy the deficiency and waste, and garner so hopeful a crop. In the absence of a stimulus to keep them up to the mark, the natives were growing oscitant. An agropnotic was necessary to rouse them, and it was prescribed and administered in the form of the marvellous society of the Ntambwe Bwanga above-mentioned, constituted expressly with the intention of gathering into a solid mass elements lopped off from other bodies and too valuable to be allowed to lie fallow. It emphasizes all the weaknesses and all the aspirations of the natives regardless of their baseness; their envy of the whites and their desire for emulation, which it feeds through their remarkable psittacism. It affords opportunity for dressing-up and mimicry, for mercenariness, love of debauchery, the passion for shows, luxury, epicurism and ghoulish rites, besides the glory of terrorizing the rest of the population. It offers the advantage of a solidarity that will be unbroken against insult, of protection against punishment, and a united front for attack.

The Ntambwe Bwanga Society

The object of the society is to provide a native understudy for all known white men whether in Belgium or the colony itself, or in whatever way connected with it, from the Head of the State, to all the ministers, and such other individuals that they hear of directly or indirectly as interesting themselves in the Congo, and all the white men, from His Excellency the Governor, down to the humblest and poorest white man in the colony.

The fetish of this society is called the Ntambwe Bwanga, and consists of the long tip of an eland's horn or of a small sausage-shaped bundle covered with lizard's skin. Wrapped up fancifully according to the caprice of its owner, it is kept in a box together with a pipe and a book in Kiswahili, in ironic homage to the white man's needs and foibles. It is supposed to represent the essence of the white man. The holder of the fetish is called the Mwine Ntambwe, and is obliged to display it at every request for curing sickness or giving advice in time of difficulty or danger. The Mwine

THE SEETHING AFRICAN POT

Ntambwe is very cleverly protected from undue inconvenience by a stringent rule establishing that the fetish may only be displayed ceremonially, and only before a quorum of not less than a stated number; and that every person present at the solemnity must immediately offer a minimum contribution of one franc in coin. This measure provides a very substantial emolument for the Mwine Ntambwe, while damping the ardour of many suppliants who might be tempted to crowd in more freely if there were no restraining conditions attached to the pleasure. As it is up to the petitioner for the graces of the Ntambwe Bwanga to provide himself with sufficient escort to support him, this slight tax sometimes makes it not so easy to collect the escort at a moment's notice.

As soon as the fetish is out of its receptacle the members of the society assume the personifications allotted to them. One may be His Excellency the Governor, another Dr. So-and-So or the foreman at some works, while servants often understudy their masters. They are addressed in appropriate terms. Apparently the Mwine Ntambwe must be a married man, for now his wife, the Mandamo, takes a hand in the proceedings, fantastically garbed in what is her own idea of a rich white woman in reception dress. Primarily she must have a highly-trimmed hat, with feathers, ribbons and flowers, and a silk or sequined costume of striking colouring and design. She chalks her face, arms, hands and feet white, and puts a tuft of curly dark feathers in the armpits. The native woman's body is almost entirely glabrous, and in her efforts at gentility she hastens to correct nature in a detail that her white sister discreetly prefers to obliterate.

At this point Mandamo [1] is seized by the spirit of the Ntambwe Bwanga and gets into a sort of frenzy, during which she is bound to interpret in Kiswahili the wishes and decisions of the fetish. In case of illness she will prescribe a cure, and it will be carried out. In case of danger she will give instructions for escaping from it. After delivering her verdict she will invariably demand offerings of food and drink, very often of presents, which will immediately be supplied by the people present. On principle she will demand everything that in their experience the natives know a white man would want: fowls, eggs, fruit, drinks, etc. The Mwine Ntambwe is bound to keep a table and set it out with fine napery, cutlery, plates and glass, such as a white man of high estate would like for his own use; the Ntambwe Bwanga is laid among the victuals, nobody daring to occupy the chair which is ceremoniously set before the laid place. All present then partake freely of the ensuing feast.

[1] Probably a contraction of Madame, a title simply prefixed to the husband's assumed white name.

There are three degrees of the Ntambwe Bwanga, which are, from the lowest upwards: Ntambwe ya Katenga, Ntambwe ya Muzunga and Ntambwe ya Baleko. The monetary admission fee is the same for all three, as members must enter the lowest order first and then climb up, but there is a vast difference in the initiation at the different stages. The fee is 400 francs in all, cash down, 100 on inscribing one's name, and 300 for the preparation of the medicine to be drunk at the initiation ceremony. It may seem an enormous sum, but it is lightly paid and natives who do not possess it easily find it on credit. For it is a very profitable investment, as they can easily earn it back on the proceeds of the nefarious practices they will share in, even while remaining in the lower orders of the society. Of course all who join do so in the hope of promotion to the fun and prestige of the higher ranks. As a matter of fact the Ntambwe Bwanga seems never to refuse membership. All is fish that comes to its net, and though individuals are carefully chosen before being promoted, it is necessary to have in the lowest order crowds that can be ordered about and put to many uses, and that provide besides handsome replenishments of the exchequer. The Katenga are the clearing-house for undesirables and incapables. They are limited to partaking only in the mass celebrations of certain rites and functions, and are denied admittance into the secrets and plans of the society, though they share in ventures congenial to their souls, and in plunders and banquets under the protection of their superior orders.

The Ntambwe ya Muzunga are drafted from the Katenga order, and must be dancers and charm-makers. As such they give performances of their own Tambwe dances to attract likely people, and join in gatherings of all sorts given by the respectable citizens, mixing with them and spying on them in order to discover victims for further ventures of the society. The Muzungu also are denied participation in the direction of the affairs of the society or in its secrets, but they are admitted to rites and functions denied to the Katenga degree, to which they are far superior while still being far removed from the highest rank.

The Ntambwe ya Baleko are the élite, the directors or generals of the society, and are quite a small and chosen body, mostly all possessors of the Ntambwe Bwanga or fetish. They burn their boats, because there is a complicated initiation ceremony to which they are only admitted after immolating a very near relation, to whom a special poison is given. They rule the society with a rod of iron, and their will is law, though in a few cases at least Muzungu members have been known to hold the fetish, possibly those already marked for promotion. The president revels in the assumed name of the Roi Albert, now probably Roi Léopold. He is assisted by a whole court bearing formerly only Belgian names, but since the expansion of the society in Angola, including Portuguese ones. Since, however, to the display-loving melanic mind a king is higher than a mere president, the commander invariably takes the name of king, accepting presidents and governors merely as councillors. Besides the general administration of the society he is supposed to preside at all initiations, but as that would be impossible considering the vastness of the territory in which the society flourishes, many observers have formed the considered opinion that there are probably two or more natives bearing the same name, acting as understudies to the president, to lighten him of some of his duties, in imitation of the deputies they have seen white authorities send out to represent them on various occasions. The extraordinary rapidity with which the Roi Albert has been known to appear at far distant places in an inconceivably short time confirms the theory of duplicate or triplicate personifications when such are necessary.

The Baleko have an astonishing knowledge of the properties of the medicinal plants growing in the country and are charged with preparing an exhalation, the secret of which they zealously guard, that enables them, sometimes from outside the habitation, to anæsthetize sleeping people without waking them, long enough to allow all their belongings to be carried off. The gravity of this proceeding is shown by the fact that sometimes their victims have recovered consciousness to find themselves shivering on the bare ground, all their possessions removed, perhaps in a lorry. This has been repeatedly the fate of lonely storekeepers, and in some cases, where barred doors or watchdogs were insurmountable obstacles to burglary, the theft has been effected by introducing a stout iron hook, fastened to a cane or pole according to the weight it had to carry, which was pushed through an upper casement or the smashed panel of a door. The drugged person suffers from a splitting headache for some days before the action of the fumes passes completely off, but no case is known to have been fatal.

Members travel frequently, and whenever they arrive they are received by the local members of the sect with the ceremony belonging to their assumed dignity. This is done in great secrecy, usually at night, so that an official or other white man notices nothing strange, and never imagines that while he is being entertained in a decorous sederunt by a white host his retinue is being regaled with the state that is due to them, usually corresponding to his own rank, by the blacks in that district and its vicinity. Every festivity is held at the house or under the auspices of the Mwine Ntambwe in the neighbourhood, and entails the showing of the Bwanga with banquets and dancing, and the offering of presents to the visitor according to his adopted title, to the accompaniment of speeches and invocations for the speedy termination of Bula Matadi, or as the society calls it, Bumbulamatadi—the Belgian rule. The "king" has repeatedly been reported to express his confidence at having under his control an obedient corps of well-trained workers ready and desirous to try their mettle on the white oppressor and to destroy him with their arms and by means of their huge reserves of poison. Lest any reader should imagine that it is the author's intention to persist in delusions and in fantastic sadistic suspicions, it may be as well to mention here the timely discovery at the end of December 1932 at S. Paul's of Loanda of a plot to poison the whole white population on the following New Year's Day. The discovery was due to the accidental overhearing of a conversation between one of his native servants and a strange native by a Portuguese gentleman who raised the alarm in time. Poison was discovered to be in process of distribution to the servants of all the white people in the town and district. It was to be administered in their food on the morrow, and further steps were to be taken to make sure of success by poisoning the water supply of the town. The police acted quickly, thereby saving some thousand people from being murdered wholesale, and the arrest of a band of fifty terrorist negroes with the witch-doctor who was at the head of the plot made the place safe for the moment.

Apart from the political purpose underlying the creation of this new terroristic association as an unsuspected weapon in the preparation of a Xenophobic rising throughout Africa at a time when all white governments are believed to be cooperating loyally to subdue and destroy these societies, its local object is the perpetration of murder, theft, and the celebration of the most horrible and revolting practices. In this respect it is, as has already been stated, a substitute for those societies which the natives temporarily abandon when going to work, and it forms an organization powerful enough to protect its members almost to the extent of immunity. In the rare cases of arrest, it pays for the best defence obtainable, and lays down any sum, at times amounting to many thousands of francs, where fines are imposed. Incidentally it has proved an inducement to natives to leave their tribal homes more willingly than they did before this attraction was provided for them, but it is hardly likely that it was planned with the ultimate purpose of furnishing labour. The terror the society inspires is so great that resistance is seldom offered to it, and members are only very exceptionally denounced by their victims for fear of reprisals, even when the identity of the culprit is certain and the sufferer is within reach of the law.

* * * * *

It is now time to give a cursory glance to the warlike secret societies that further deepen the gloom and add to the dangers of African life—the life that stay-at-home Europeans love to picture to themselves as one of idyllic happiness for the primitive native undisturbed by the tide of progress and civilization.

These secret societies of Xenophobic proclivities always rest on a religious basis, of a pagan but not Christian character. They are not merely political associations.

They never have any dealings with Ethiopianism as this is a term applied to the unorthodox native Christian churches and sects, for which they have a perfect horror. The one and only bond between the two categories of rebels lies in their common loathing for the white man, and it is this that has induced in them a desultory collaboration, in the hope of arriving at the ultimate goal of wiping him from the land.

Too much stress must not be laid on the word collaboration, for it might lead to the misapprehension of supposing that they in some way support each other on the field of action. Indeed, their attitude is rather one of platonic and distant approval of their respective aims, so that they bury their differences and avoid an antagonism

SECRET SOCIETIES OF CENTRAL AFRICA

that would weaken their forces by internecine strife. Though refusing to work jointly, they may be said to work concurrently.

African chiefs assume the rule by various means; by inheritance, by nomination of the council of elders, or by abreption of the office. In the case of inheritance they have to defend it against disappointed rivals and would-be usurpers or, as was quite commonly the case in former days, on the death of the chief all his sons fought among themselves for the post, and the devil took the hindmost. Or a victorious warrior pushed his claim so successfully as to overcome all legitimate competition. Whatever the road to power, the new ruler's first care, besides ridding himself of dangerous competitors, is that of capturing the support of the witch-doctors and getting himself proclaimed by them as the approved candidate of all the spirits, by pretty much the same means as the leaders of Ethiopianism have to do.

The Bantu tribes have no taste for selenology or astrology, and never get an innocent crick in their necks by studying the mysterious courses of the heavenly orbs. They demand a sterner preparation for their witch-doctors, and many young pupils succumb to the rigour of their training, either being drowned while testing their magical powers in a hole at the bottom of a river, or in some other equally risky act of endurance expected of them as a result of their schooling, before they are qualified in the profession, by a board of practitioners, as invested with supernatural attributes. The grimness of their procedure for soothsaying is only commensurate with the hardships of their apprenticeship; brutal disregard of suffering is the keynote of their calling.

By whatever means he reached the chieftainship, once installed, the chief's authority is absolute, and he is faithfully obeyed. Until he decides to break the peace there is no war, and when he decides there shall be war the tribe rises unquestioningly and follows him out against all odds, to fight as long as he commands, and to sink into quiet at his bidding, or that of his successor if he dies. When he is obliged to have generals under him, or to split his army, any one of the under leaders who is more daring or more lucky stands a good chance of ousting him, if he has the support of the witch-doctor, as the tribe will believe him the man more favoured by the tribal spirits. Sometimes fortunate warriors who did not dare to face the old chief will seize power at his death if he has no heir of sufficient personal prestige for whom the tribe will fight.

The chief must always lead fights in person, for the prestige of a fighting chief or of a rebel leader depends on his daring, his courage, his hairbreadth escapes, his rapidity in striking, and his ruthlessness. His name must become a byword and he must keep his followers keyed up to the highest pitch by continual action. If he can start the legend of being invulnerable, of mysteriously appearing and disappearing, or of passing unseen in the midst of the enemy, or do anything to prove supernatural gifts and to confirm the idea that he has been chosen by the spirits and will be protected by them, he will become a national hero, and with trembling limbs and love for him in their hearts, the tribe will fight for him, and after his death his spirit will be a tribal spirit to be called on by all people.[1]

Serious difficulties arise when there are under-chiefs with a paramount tribal chief over them. In theory the paramount chief has the command over all his land and people, but in practice the local chief has higher authority in his own district. He must transmit the orders of his paramount, but for his own people his will and not the paramount's has value. In civil war they will stand up for him against the paramount, but if he has not their support he must flee.

Nabingi or Nya-Bingi [2]

The Nabingi, or Nya-Bingi, meaning Mother of Wealth, Mother of Expellers, is a very potent secret society apparently born in the Ruanda, Ndorwa and East Congo territories. The origin of the society is not known, but students of Africa

[1] See Appendix II, the Wahele rebellion.
[2] Due to the courtesy of T.P.

who have examined its features do not think it commands the same antiquity as the cannibalistic societies already described. Its whole aspect is that of a fanatical sect, revolutionary in method and anarchic in effect, as opposed to the liberal and religious principles of the indigenous Kubandua cult. This latter is an established monotheistic faith traditionally allied to and co-operating with the Native Government, unopposed to education and progress, insisting upon social as well as religious duties, wielding a wholesome influence on tribal morality and finally uniting in religious equality three races of different origin.

Apparently the Nabingi society has a secret language but it is seldom obligatory; discipline is lax, moral obligations are almost dispensed with. Fees for "services rendered," such as procuring medicinal herbs, preparing poisons and philtres for curses and black magic, are extremely heavy compared to the tariffs of other local native practitioners. By means of an unusually developed form of witchcraft in which hypnotic suggestion plays a leading part, the country within its sphere of operations is completely terrorized. Owing to the swift vengeance of the society upon traitors or informers it is only by means of endless tact and secrecy that reliable information can be obtained. The elements of fanaticism among Nabingi adherents and terrorism of those who are not, render every local native at least unreliable and provide a refuge for the cult. Thus ideal means and conditions are created for fomenting the organization of rebellion, and most serious feature of all, absolute secrecy is ensured. Whole populations become supernaturally terrorized willy-nilly, chiefly nilly; every village is a secret food store for the Nabingi; every man, woman and child an involuntary spy against authority. Alien political agents are found usually grossly misinformed except on certain spectacular points of ceremonial.

The densely populated country is one of precipitous mountains, lava caves and often forests marked on the maps as "impenetrable" or "trackless," or "uninhabitable"; besides, these forests are intersected by international frontiers across which pursuing troops may not pass. The police of the respective governments are reduced to the uningenious plan of waiting until the Nabingi become bold enough to form bands for mass attack, the news of which takes some days to reach a European post. When any troops are finally sent out in pursuit they may find smoking villages and rotting bodies, but the leader of the expedition has long before given the word for dispersal and the aggressors disappeared individually, fading into the forests, quite "penetrable" to naked natives who know the few winding tracks like their own hands.

Nabingi apostles are male and female, and

claim to be, and are regarded by the population as being, possessed by the "Spirit," and an official report says:

"There is no shadow of doubt that they do exercise remarkable supernatural powers when under 'possession.' It is also currently alleged that the Nabingi spirit can transfer itself, that its voice is heard in houses which are suddenly visited by it. Certain it is that those who feel or believe themselves to be 'possessed' have thenceforth abnormal power."

It is beyond the scope of these notes to make a detailed examination of the religious beliefs of the Nabingi; it is sufficient to mention that it apparently recognizes a single deity, Imana, and has no fetish in the sense of that of some other secret societies. Instead it has made a completely new departure from local custom by adopting a living White Sheep as the sacred emblem of the cult, an institution probably due to the influence of the Christian emblem of the Lamb. However, the Sacred White Sheep is not known to have especial religious significance attached to it, and is not worshipped, but rather is thought to be a sign of office, that all apostles and leaders take round with them, and for which, as for themselves, they claim complete invulnerability from physical injury. The miraculous escapes of some of the apostles and of their White Sheep from what seemed certain death has greatly contributed to establishing faith in the society.

SECRET SOCIETIES OF CENTRAL AFRICA

The first manifestation of the Nabingi apostle in an area to which he or she is attached is given in a way to establish the supernatural prestige of the society. So many are the authenticated instances of people suddenly seized with acute physical ailments within forty-eight hours after having incurred the displeasure of an apostle that any sudden, acute pain is commonly referred to as "Nabingi anounve"—"Nabingi has cursed me," while many cases of the healing of initiates from physical affliction rapidly following the curses of apostles upon unenthusiastic adherents point to a recognized, though elementary, use of suggestion. Every act is studiously invested with supernatural significance.

People unversed in African psychology may doubt this statement, for it is hard to believe that any person enjoying perfect health should have such absolute faith in the abstract power of a curse, and die of no other malady than the belief that certain people are invested with the mysterious authority of commanding death. Yet African psychology is scarcely more than a modification of white psychology, for if white people rarely carry their conviction of having to die to the point of actual death, by the tens of thousands they have faith in miraculous cures, and benefit by them, as the briskness of trade at innumerable shrines amply testifies. Africans are famous for recovering miraculously from appalling wounds, without any, or with only the slightest and most rudimentary assistance, in an incredibly short time; but with a curse, a downright outspoken curse hurled at them by the proper person, they just wilt, deprived of their hold on life. An incident officially reported by a Native Commissioner in the Ruanda district will very aptly serve both to illustrate the workings of primitive minds and to explain the methods of the Nabingi society for establishing its authority.

"In March 1919, when I was on an Anglo-Belgian patrol, the Nabingi movement threatened by various overt signs to assume fresh activity. The priestess Kaigirirwa entered Kigezi one day at dawn on a mission from the south. Passing through one of the first villages in British territory, she hailed a man called Sabaza who was mending a spear in front of his rather isolated house, while his small flock of sheep and goats were grazing close by. She gave him the usual salutation, 'Amasho' (literally, I wish you cattle). 'Give me a fat sheep,' she added, 'for tribute.' The man answered roughly without paying much attention, asking what a woman needed with a sheep (they are taboo as food in Ruanda) and bade her be off. She instantly replied, 'Who are you not to grant recognition? I am Nabingi (possessed). Tomorrow before this time, you will not need your flock.'

"His son found me at dusk camped on the border hills. He explained the news. His father had gone into the house, perhaps wisely, and refused to move. His wife was guarding him at the house. The boy assured me that from his point of view there was nothing to be done. If soldiers came, he argued, the neighbours would say they had killed him. I sent the boy home with instructions to admit no one, and that no outside food should be introduced into the house at least till the next evening, as the poisoning of milk is a much developed art. While we were still talking I spoke to the Sudanese sergeant-major, and in Arabic (which the boy did not understand) gave orders for three reliable men who knew the local language to follow the boy separately and to conceal themselves that night close by, and on three sides of the house, to watch till the following morning. The moon was bright. I could not spare more than three men from the next day's operations, which were to begin before dawn. The boy left, and I also sent down a local chief of another clan, to make discreet inquiries on the spot, without telling him the details we had heard. He returned just before dawn with entirely corroborative evidence of all the details, and with the discouraging opinion that 'a Nabingi curse did not let live a second day.'

"The following afternoon, when still on the march, one of the soldiers returned to report. 'No one had left or entered the hut all night, nor in the morning. The boy had gone back straight home from our camp. The wife had come out and wailed before noon. She announced to heaven that the Nabingi spirit had spoken from the inner room that Sabaza's hour had come, and . . . that he was already dead.'"

Undoubtedly, however, the Nabingi society had already established its rule over its native haunts long before it was invited to join in the anti-white campaign then taking hold, though many years passed before its connection with many rebellions that broke out in regions far removed from it was understood, and the white authorities awoke to the fact that there was a unity of direction and method behind them all. When at last the society rose to fame it had extended to many neighbouring districts, and its success was due to its newly-appointed fighting leader, whose tribal name was Bichu-Birenga, meaning Clouds Roll By, and nicknamed Ndochibiri, or N'Toki Mbili, meaning Two Fingers. He was a Congolese Muhundu, and he owed his nickname to the fact of having lost all but the thumb and forefinger of his left hand. Like so many other successful native leaders, N'Toki Mbili was an epileptic, and in one of the attacks of his malady had fallen into a camp-fire and been severely burnt before being rescued. He also bore curious deep scars on his chest, by some supposed to be the outcome of a similar misadventure, while others alleged that he had been struck by lightning.

He had a fighting leader's physique, being of awesome presence with wild fanatical eyes and filed teeth, and habitually wore attached to his necklet of charms the backsights of nine rifles, being those, according to his claim, of soldiers killed with his own hands, and a goat's drinking-horn that is known to have contained the blood of at least two Europeans. He was a born leader; intrepid, resourceful, intelligent, endowed with a really notable psychic force and with those other qualities that constitute the peculiar personality of a guerilla warfare leader. He is an outstanding figure among the many African rebel chiefs for qualities that would have distinguished him at any time and in any land. From a small and comparatively local band of rebels such as it was when he took over command, under his generalship the Nabingi extended its influence down to what was then German West Africa, whose Herrera revolt, started in 1903, lasting desultorily for years, and the Tanganyika Maji-Maji rebellion of 1905 to 1907 were later both attributed to his instigations.

At that time he had two headquarters, one in Bwitwa, Congo Belge, and the other at Mysoro, German Ruanda, from which ordained apostles were sent out for propaganda and to collect the tithes exacted by the society.

The Tanganyika or Maji-Maji Rebellion

The Tanganyika rebellion broke out in August 1905 in the Kilwa district with the murder of a German planter and his Arab servants, but it had been brewing for some time entirely unnoticed. It followed close on the Herrera rebellion which had begun in 1903, and was not then quite suppressed. Both of these events were later attributed to Nabingi influence though at the time they

THE SEETHING AFRICAN POT

happened nobody suspected the connection with a secret society operating in such distant countries as Ruanda and the Congo. It was known however that the Herrera had sent encouraging and loving messages from across the Continent. Both Tanganyika and what was then called German West Africa being under the same rule, the exchange between the two colonies facilitated easy intercourse between the natives, so no great weight was given to the fact.

The natives had laid their plans carefully, in such complete secrecy that nobody, civil servants, officers, police, traders or missionaries had the least inkling of the storm about to burst, and everybody was taken unawares.

As usual, the witch-doctors took a prominent part by dispensing miraculous medicine. They circulated the story that a famous witch-doctor who was supposed to have recently departed life, had instead transferred himself to the Rufigi River, in whose water he lived in the semblance of a water monster, disporting himself by splashing about. They assured the natives that complete invulnerability from the effects of the white man's arms, and invisibility at the moment of capture, was promised to those men, women and children alike, who went on pilgrimage to the Rufigi River and got sprayed by the water monster. When public desire was roused to a proper pitch they circulated a modified version of the first tale that said how, aware of the impossibility for most people of going on a pilgrimage to his residence, the water-demon patriotically condescended to distribute his spray to his colleagues still in the flesh, to be by them passed on for a consideration to whomsoever chose to apply for it. All the natives did so, some asking to be sprinkled with it, others instead preferring to carry some hung about their persons in pieces of hollowed bamboo cane.

The first important clash was at the German inland post of Liwale, in the Kilwa district, which was attacked, taken and destroyed by an overwhelming force, the hordes yelling "Maji-Maji!" which in Kiswahili means "Water, water!" as they charged. Hence the name of Maji-Maji rebellion.

While the puzzled Germans were investigating the peculiar war-cry, the wounded and the families of the slain were complaining to the witch-doctors about the inefficacy of the charm supplied them, for neither had the guns spurted water as promised, nor had the bullets turned to a cooling spray which they had been solemnly assured was its alternative effect. Naturally the witch-doctors had their answers pat. Either the men had been bewitched by some wizardry more powerful than the charm, a fact of everyday occurrence in Africa, or else they had turned to look back over their shoulders, an act that would infallibly break the charm. Some even went the length of assuring the complainants that the fallen were not dead, but merely resting after their fight, and would soon arise again. The replies restored confidence; the population got itself sprinkled anew, and the aggressiveness of the warriors was notably increased, as not one of them dared look back after such a warning.

Fighting now spread to most districts of the colony; and the Germans sent to Papuasia and Melanesia for their coloured troops to quell the rebellion. Quite a number of Germans were killed too, among them a bishop, two nuns and two lay brothers, who with foolhardiness and mistaken religious zeal threw themselves before the natives to implore them to return to their homes. The worst of the rebellion was in the districts of Mahenge, Ininga and Songea, and though within six months the remainder of the colony was quiet, in those three districts peace was not restored till early in 1907, after a ruthless repression entailing the destruction of all the crops and all the villages in the disaffected areas. The native death-roll was not perhaps so high among the fighters, but in all, including the victims of the ensuing famine, it rose to the ghastly number of 120,000.

However, there was no visible depreciation in the value of charms, nor was the reputation of surviving witch-doctors at all dimmed by the failure of their medicine. For such is the native mind. To return to the Nabingi.

In 1911 the apprehension of Myhumusa, the Ruanda Nabingi priestess according to her own description, which, according to official report, checked the propaganda for an anti-white crusade under Nabingi direction, and the scenes of her activities had peace for about a year. She was taken as a political deportee to Uganda, where she was always delighted to talk to anybody who could speak her own language. When she had been finally captured, after a protracted conflict, her carrying-chair was found to be riddled with bullets and herself quite calm and unperturbed. Subsequently trouble broke out again, for on the death or deportation of each apostle or local personification of the Nabingi cult another representative became possessed of the spirit.

"It is a remarkable fact that during the war, despite the presence of Anglo-Belgian forces with artillery in British Ruanda, the militant activities of the Nabingi Society increased enormously," states an official report. They were equally directed against British, Belgians and Germans as opportunity arose. The caravans of the Missions des Pères Blancs were attacked in the Mlera district, German patrols were murdered in the Kivu area, Belgian lines of communication were cut. Rebellion was organized in the newly-formed district of Kigezi. In January 1915 N'Toki M'Bili with some two thousand fanatics and accompanied by his Sacred White Sheep, stormed Chaliafi Fort, held by Anglo-Belgian troops, a few days after a strong German attack had been repulsed. The Nabingi assault was pressed for some five hours in the face of heavy machine-gun fire up the only slope unprotected by the lake or dense thorn bush. The attack retired as night fell, after capturing three rifles and ammunition; the Sacred White Sheep defeated all attempts at marksmanship at comparatively short range.

This was one of N'Toki M'Bili's most spectacular exploits, but not the only one, nor was he the only leader to escape being hit under heavy fire; many apostles were also known to have made incredible escapes; in these conditions the name of N'Toki M'Bili and of the Nabingi Society became a whispered terror over an immense area of Central Africa, and their authority practically undisputed by the natives.

In January 1917 an Anglo-Belgian punitive expedition under the Commissioner of Police of Uganda failed to moderate the zeal of the society or to "scotch" the fighting leader. Says another report, "The difficulties are such as to almost negative any military proposition. A vicious circle of spies surrounds the slightest movements of any military force."

To secure his position N'Toki M'Bili contracted an alliance with the family of the Congolese frontier chief Itemberu by marrying the sister of Itemberu's blood brother, Birego, already a Nabingi apostle ordained at Kyante. This is a very ordinary and very binding measure generally resorted to in Africa, and in consequence of it he was able, with the aid of the Nabingi priestess Kaigirirwa and her Mukiga husband, Luhemba, to organize in 1917 a rebellion in the Rukigi country. As a rebellion it was pretty much as all the others. However, one episode of it is especially noteworthy, for in August 1917 Bichubirenga, at the head of 1600 followers, was able to approach unreported within half an hour of Kabale station and remain there two days without a breath of his presence reaching the Commissioner, no suspicion whatever of disaffection or unrest, despite the personal dislike with which the society was regarded by a great part of the Wakiga. Apparently information of some sort about his previous motions had leaked out, which he rightly or wrongly attributed to a group of natives living in a small village just beyond Kabale station. At dawn on the 12th of August he attacked it, and sixty-three alien native settlers and government agents were massacred. Although the victims had either wives or blood brothers among the local population, no warning had reached them of this impending fate. The population showed signs of sympathy with the Nabingi.

Early in 1919 a clan of Bu-Hundu natives belonging to N'Toki M'Bili's own tribe dissociated themselves from their redoubtable clansman's policy, and for safety abandoned their ancestral home, moved across the border and founded their little alien colony in British territory, perching their village on a rock north of Lake Mutanda. The Nabingi chief deeply resented this as an insult and decided to avenge it. He began by allying himself with the Batwa, the malignant pygmy archers and hunters, and with a band of them marched over the frontier by night, surprised the village at dawn and wiped out all its male inhabitants. The Batwa murdered the children in cold blood and carried off the women, who were not ill-treated. The raiding band then dispersed and faded individually as usual into unadministered territory, where it was physically and politically impossible to follow them.

In April 1919 a Nabingi priest established himself alone on the northern slopes of Muhavura, on the 10th, attacking with three hundred followers the Government roadworks. This expedition met with disaster and he was lodged in gaol on the 13th. On June 5th N'Toki M'Bili returned secretly to Kisslu and foregathered with Itemberu, Birego, Kaigirirwa and Luhemba. Nabingi support was invoked, Nabingi rites and sacrifices performed. Information that had discreetly trickled down suddenly stopped for a few days, but finally news was sent that the rebels were in a particular spot, and almost immediately afterwards one of his messengers was stopped in the forest. That gave a clue to the party's whereabouts, and as was subsequently learnt, N'Toki M'Bili had crossed into British territory with five hundred followers, accompanied also by the priestess Kaigirirwa, and had camped in the Kayonsa forest, through which the frontier runs. Leaving the bulk of his band under the care of Kaigirirwa, N'Toki M'Bili, Luhemba and some other ten leading rebels emerged and proceeded through Kumba to about ten miles south with the object of organizing a general rising and of striking the first blow at the open station of Kabale. The Kayonsa forest was as far as possible surrounded on the Belgian (west) side by Belgian patrols, on the north, east and south sides by a cordon of native agent's followers and Uganda police. The richly stocked Luemba (S.E.) corner of the forest was left open, and ostensibly unguarded, as a trap, into which N'Toki M'Bili unwarily walked. Either through a misplaced sense of security, but quite possibly out of contempt for danger, he had grown casual in his usual precautions, for on the night of June 23rd the party's fires in a deserted spot aroused suspicion, and led to their being tracked down and wiped out. Surrounded on all sides, and with all his followers fallen, N'Toki M'Bili could not have escaped being taken prisoner; rather than which he hanged himself to the branch of a tree. When his body was cut down it was discovered that no bullet had struck him in spite of the heavy fire that had been directed upon him. The Sacred White Sheep which had been continually close to him during the fight was also found at the foot of the tree perfectly unharmed. It was taken to Kabale and publicly killed, and its body down to the last hair consumed by fire before an assembled crowd of natives on July 3rd. Luhemba himself, mortally wounded, dragged himself to a near hut, which was tracked and surrounded. To gain time Luhemba threw some ammunition on a fire; then he threw a rope over one of the beams of the hut, broke his rifle, and swung himself to his death. The body was cut down immediately, but life was extinct. The rest of the band was traced and surprised and all taken prisoners. Kaigirirwa was tried before the Baraza (court) at Buzene. A report of the trial says:

"The woman is an extraordinary character. By dint of years of training she has acquired a falsetto voice, and professes inability to walk normally, her method of progression being on tiptoe in a crouching position with the aid of two sticks, the resemblance, except as regards dress, to the pictorial and juvenile concepts of old-time witches in Europe being most striking. During the course of the Baraza it was interesting to note the effect she produced on the assembled natives. The chiefs, with scarcely an exception, trembled whenever her look was directed towards them. She also made most noticeable efforts to exercise some form of hypnotism over me (the English magistrate who was trying her). She was captured with her whole stock-in-trade, which, with the exception of some spears of unusual construction, was publicly burnt at the Baraza."

It was then ascertained that she had already once before been deported from Uganda owing to her disturbing and pernicious influence over the more ignorant natives, about ten years before.

This letter to the British Museum, accompanying N'Toki M'Bili's skull, published by kind permission of the Museum and the author,[1] takes up the tale:

"When Bichubirenga was finally disposed of, so firm was the general belief in his invulnerability and fame, as well as in the supernatural powers of the Nabingi, that practically no one would believe in the fact of his death. I summoned two or three chiefs within a day's journey of Kabale to view the bodies, but burial in the tropics must be on the same day, and he would not keep for general inspection. And yet some proof of death was most essential, for the restoration of peace and confidence for a new era, both in British and neighbouring territories. So the N'Toki M'Bili [2] were cut off at the wrist, preserved in salt and arsenic, and then hung up by a string outside my office

[1] T.P.—U.M.I.R., June 1922.
[2] The crippled hands.

window. There, when I left, they still swung gracefully to the fickle breezes of Kabale, shown tactfully as a *memento mori* to any suspected associates when they called on business.... What remained of Bichubirenga was given decent burial in a carefully selected and secluded spot as befitted a great guerilla leader.

"One of the furthest sources of the Nile rises close below him. One day when at my fishpond I found a new and well-trodden track passing up the station hill, apparently to nowhere. I followed it; the tracks led to N'Toki M'Bili's grave. They circled round it and returned. Next day I set up an unobtrusive watcher above upon the hillside to see what manner of men the pathmakers might be. A week passed and not a soul had been observed. Then I changed my tactics; alone with a faithful orderly I hid near the grave at night and watched. About midnight, when the mist was densest and most piercing, the sound of bare feet approached. Some three-score black forms loomed out of the mist and grouped themselves slowly round the grave. They seemed to whisper softly some sort of set formula. With that the party disappeared innocuously into the night leaving no trace behind.... The visitors, I found, were aliens from 'abroad.' They harboured ambitious feelings for a 'Nabinga irredenta' and for the re-establishment of the 'good old days.' It had been prophesied that the head of N'Toki M'Bili would be the future symbol to revive the spirit—the honour and power and the glory—of the fighting leadership. The head they had planned should be abstracted at the next Saturnalian festival. Then the

European would finally be driven out, and with him labour for them and taxation. The next night, two hours before dawn, Musa (the only phlegmatic unbeliever I could trust in this somewhat gruesome task) and I proceeded with spade in hand and walking delicately, up along the waters of the infant Nile. We dug, longer than I had thought possible or pleasing, till metal struck the bone. We removed the skull and tied the jaw with string. We filled in the grave, recovered it quite naturally and departed. Carrying the skull in my left hand and the spade in my right, we were careful to return home by another way. The skull we hid for the night in my laundry-basket. We were afraid of its being discovered in any obscurer place. Next night we boiled the head and cleaned it tidily.... N'Toki M'Bili was despatched to the coast on its way to the British Museum in a wooden box by a tall mail-runner carrying the postal packet balanced on his head, blowing gaily upon his shrill reed whistle, all unconscious of the load he carried. Had he known, the simple superstitious fellow would doubtless have uttered a piercing howl as if he had been bitten, and considered himself cursed, and rendered up his ghost soon after.

"N'Toki M'Bili's drinking-horn has held human blood, including that of at least two Europeans. The necklet and regalia of the Nabingi were captured one night when we arrived uninvited at a well-attended rendezvous."

At the time of N'Toki M'Bili's death an official estimate of the Nabingi society was as follows:

THE SEETHING AFRICAN POT

"The probable diffusion of the Nabingi ranges from coast to coast of the African Continent. Its centre lies about ex-German Ruanda, now a Belgian mandate, British East Africa, the Congo Basin, thereby including Belgian and French Congo, and Angola, with manifest sympathy in the Empire of Ethiopia that may result any day in active participation. One must remember that in Ethiopia there are the leading tribes that prey on the lower ones, 'illtreating, robbing them and raiding them for slavery.'

"The Nabingi with real faith and conviction, the organizers, the leaven that leaveneth the whole lump, are really few. In time of crisis or rebellion the terror of them, their witchcraft and curses are capable of stirring up 90 per cent of the population. The masses live in the centre of the Continent, but their agents live in the towns, especially of South Africa."

N'Toki M'Bili's death proved a momentary check to the activities of the society, but as early as September 1920 a report from British Ruanda gave warning that one Ruchezi, alias Kitumu, was giving himself out as the successor of the dead chief and going about with a white sheep and a small band of followers, in consequence of which the frontier population south-west of Lake Burrajoni were said to have fled from their homes.

It would be tedious and excessive to dedicate much further attention to the Nabingi; however, it is necessary to say that the society in time completely recovered its loss, and blossomed forth with renewed energy, and still holds the limelight in Central Africa. The Kwango revolt, of which more will be said, seems to be due to its direction, and certainly quantities of raids and many of the border incidents in Kenya, Sudan, etc., are fruits of its tree. In 1929 an important rebellion broke out in Belgian Ruanda led by a brother of Musinga, the two being reported in the Belgian press as brothers of a Nabingi priestess. In the Gatsibu district some chiefs and their tribesmen were murdered and their villages pillaged. Troops were sent out against them, but according to their time-honoured tactics, the assailants had taken refuge in British territory. They were, however, captured, Musinga's brother among them, and delivered over to the Belgians. As their sister is said to be a political prisoner of the British and to be detained in Uganda, she is probably Kaigirirwa. Measures in collaboration with the British were announced to have been taken for the occupation of the Nabingi general headquarters at Kyante. For some reason or other Musinga held his place for a little while longer; however, by the end of 1933 the Belgian authorities were heartily tired of him, and on November 12th he was deposed and deported to Kamenber with his mother, his wives and younger children. He was succeeded by his eldest son, Rudalugwa, a young man who seems to be sympathetic to the authorities and to his tribe.

THE SEETHING AFRICAN POT

The Kwango Revolt of 1931

On May 21st, 1931, a Belgian official noticed how all the able-bodied men round Pukusu had quitted their villages and collected in the forest. Rumour was running of Satan's near arrival to the Kwango bringing the natives all they desired in the way of money, clothes, food, etc. In exchange he was said to expect all the natives to rid themselves of everything of European origin, including the people, and to build a hut in a forest recess with a path leading to it, where the natives could lay their offerings to him. The path was necessary because Satan meant to arrive by night in a motor.

A rapid enquiry elicited the information that the natives were effectually destroying all they held that was accounted European, such as their tax receipts, passes, and even fifty-franc notes of the Banque de Congo Belge, breaking and tearing up all they could of European origin.

The nearest administrator hurried to the scene with his four men, but was attacked by at least two hundred natives who discharged their arrows on the party. In the ensuing fray five natives were shot down and the others fled, but the little band withdrew pending reinforcements. Another official hastened to the scene with forty men, but the situation was by now so serious that all he could do was to protect the lives of the nearby

Europeans and try to prevent the movement from spreading north. The Kikwit territory was by now affected in the districts of Gombambulu, Kizungu, Congo and Bangui.

Kandale district was no less affected, where another official on his way for a holiday in Europe unexpectedly came on the natives of Kazanga collected in the forest, and he hurried back to his post. There too the rising was at Satan's instigation and the natives were destroying everything European. Meanwhile, two Government couriers had been stopped at Lukalama in the Yonge district, and a young official, M. Ballot, was despatched there, unwisely, with only one soldier as escort. At Lukalama he found that all the males had deserted the village, and he continued to Kilamba where he was threatened by a large crowd of the natives. Both men fired their guns in the air to intimidate the rebels, who instead fired a volley of arrows, one of which pierced the *nuque* of M. Ballot, who fell. The assailants then hurled themselves upon him and literally hacked his body to pieces, after horribly mutilating it.

Communications were by now interrupted between Kikwit and Kandale, and the situation of the whites became highly critical. Fortunately a *peloton* of soldiers happened to be cycling in the neighbourhood, and rumour of the rebellion reached the commanding officer, who rushed to the rescue. Even his column was insufficient to quell the revolt, but it was strong enough to guard the Europeans. Along the Lukafu, the Bwele, the Lutshima and the Kwilu rebellion had spread. At Indele and Mulua missionary schools were burnt down and the Europeans in the region threatened with murder.

The revolt extended between Banza, Kandale and Feshi, the district lying between the Kwile and Kwenge rivers, and thirteen hundred men took part in it. Detachments were sent out from all available places and a battalion five hundred strong formed, but not until June 27th did the first reinforcements begin to arrive.

In the Lutshima district fifteen hundred Bampende men answered Satan's call and followed their witch-doctors to the forests. On May 29th there was a fight in which the natives used knives, lances and arrows and a few old stone guns. Seeing the first natives shot down, the assailants began to slip away, when the intervention of the witch-doctor frenetically shaking an old box containing some of the gifts of Satan rallied them back. A second assault took place under the leadership of the doctor, who never ceased to beat on his box, but when he was shot down the attack dispersed rapidly.

The chiefs were at the head of their men. At Indele, after a fight the natives calmed down. By the end of September the revolt was practically quelled everywhere, only a few places still agitating.

It has been ascertained that the witch-doctors had instigated the revolt and that the body of M. Ballot was used for making medicine to render the rebels invulnerable. They had been promised that the balls would pass through their bodies without hurting them; the disappointment in the promised effect of the anointing probably had some weight in cooling their tempers.

However, at the bottom of the revolt was the very serious economic crisis afflicting the native unable to get work and thereby driven to despair as to how to provide money for his taxes and his needs. In this state he falls an easy and a willing prey to the witch-doctors to whom he turns for help and advice.

In 1933 the Kwango revolt, previously repressed on the surface but instead inexplicably spreading to distant districts unconnected with each other, and between which there was no communication, broke out again in an aggravated form. Correspondence in the Essort Colonial of October tell the history of it.

It began with the same symptoms that had characterized the 1931 revolt, only it was no longer in the name of Satan, but in that of a fetish called " Djinda." It broke out among the Zamba and the Gudi Kalonga and Gudi Nord villages. As already among other tribes, white goats and white fowls were killed in symbolic destruction of the white people. The Belgian official commanding the district was to be murdered, and his death represented as a hunting accident. The confidences were made to an officer who chanced to meet an ancient and devoted soldier of the 1914–18 war, who warned him to be careful. He also told how the Bawango tribe were being stirred up by witch-doctors from the Bashilele district who made a ceremonial killing of a white ram, spilling its blood on the ground. Then taking some water in their cupped hands they filled their mouths with it and blew it up into the air with great force so that it did not fall back on to the people, and explained that if the teaching of Djinda was followed the Europeans would be blown from the land as the water had been blown.

A little while later the same official was near Gudi and needed carriers, which he had always obtained with ease. He had great difficulty in procuring seven, though none in obtaining food, and the natives surrounded him in the usual way. Among them was the ancient soldier with whom he was friendly, who this time openly asked him if he knew about the attempt to be made on his life. The official replied that he did, "and not only was he prepared to defend it, but his death would not benefit the natives at all, but rather bring down severe punishment on their heads by the

Government that would avenge his death." He also reminded them of the futility of their revolts that they might remember had inevitably ended in disaster for themselves. Murdered Europeans had always been replaced and the reins of authority tightened. He advised them to desist from revolt. The natives enquired whether troops were expected, and on the affirmative answer he received the warning, always aloud and in public, that Gonde, recognized chief of the Bakwa-Kipingi had convoked all the Itanga men and those of the neighbouring villages to distribute provisions of gunpowder for use exclusively in the approaching rebellion against the white man. However, white fowls and white goats were running about the place.

Later a note was entrusted to his water-carrier informing him that the natives of Gudi had sent for Djinda, but it never reached him as it was taken from the bearer. On arriving at Gudi he noticed the disappearance of all the white fowls and goats, and an enquiry confirmed the arrival of Djinda. Except for the lack of bearers the natives were perfectly respectful. However, a certain unrest was in the air, and several people asked him about the arrival of troops. The official reported as symptomatic the presence of Djinda among natives fully advised of the failure of medicine made from the body of M. Ballot, and who, alarmed by the arrival of troops, had sent for this fetish. The xenophoby of the intention was proved without doubt.

The connection with the Nabingi was considered pretty well established by the fact that this cult for Satan followed on the footsteps of a mysterious priestess. Though she was reported as travelling about unaccompanied by any White Sheep, her tactics appeared to be the same as her predecessors had adopted, and perhaps the former emblem was suppressed as having become too notorious for safety. There was a good deal of evidence that another domestic animal had taken its place among the adepts of the society across the whole continent of Africa. This fresh development anyway deserves attention, for if not the emblem of the Nabingi, it certainly was a new departure in native behaviour and must have a meaning.

The Watu Wa Muungu

This is a new religious sect discovered early in 1934 among the younger natives of the Kikuyu tribe of Kenya. Its name means People of God, and they seem to affect epilepsy on a vast scale. Their prayers are spectacular, for they hold up their arms to the sky and mingle the cries of wild beasts of prey, such as the lion and the leopard, with their petitions, while trembling violently under the stress of their emotions.

It is a nest of fanatics, and when they began to

cause some anxiety to the white population of the Kijabe district, their conduct was officially enquired into.

A general meeting of the sect held under the paramount chief of the Kikuyu tribe on the surface seemed perfectly innocent and its purpose legal, but after it was over and the natives had dispersed, a conflict between police and raiders in the Ndarugu forest, in which three natives belonging to the sect were killed, led to the accidental discovery that Wandorobo blacksmiths were actively preparing war-arrows and spears for a future rebellion. Quite a quantity of these was discovered in a well-hidden cave, together with a store of iron arrowheads and a provision of deadly poison sufficient to smear the arrows and the spears.

As yet there has been no open hostility against the whites, but experience points out their methods as a fresh variation in the xenophobia organization of Africa, especially as rumours of a new war in Europe were found to be circulating among the natives, causing some unrest.

IV BLACK NATIONALISM FALLS INTO THE RUSSO-GERMAN TRAP

The negroes of America themselves repeated most of the same errors of judgment that they had deplored in the white man's handling of the Africans; this they never realized, and therefore they never attempted to correct their procedure. For it must be remembered that scarcely any of them had even the faintest idea of what Africa was really like, or what were the advantages and drawbacks of life out there. By 1900 the vast majority of them were the offspring of slaves, sometimes of many generations, and all they knew of the distant land of their origin was by hearsay, from stories told at the fireside or through their songs. They had made no attempt to keep up their languages. Actually, very few of them knew or cared from what part of Africa their parent stock had been torn, or to what tribes they had belonged, any more than they seemed to wish to return there when at last they were freed.

That they had been most brutally ill treated by everybody connected with the slave trade no one has ever been heartless enough to deny; but on the other hand there is no manner of doubt that very often they were bought by the kindest and most humane masters, and had a very good time of it, much better than they would have had at home, in all likelihood. There is a certain tendency to exaggerate the woes of slaves in America, for on the whole, with the exception of the most piteous cases, which could not have been general, if only from business considerations, once natives were landed in America they were much better off than if they had been caught by some neighbouring tribe at home. First of all, slaves were rarely taken from the fighting tribes of Africa owing to the difficulty of catching them, and of coping with them after they were caught; and the weaker tribes, continually raided by their neighbours in Africa, had their men wiped out or put into the cooking-pot, while the women and children were carried off to local slavery in circumstances far worse than those prevailing in America.

Slaves did not come from South Africa. The aborigines of that part of the continent were Bushmen and Hottentots who as often as not were killed on sight, but never raided for slavery, as they would not have found a market. The other inhabitants are the so-called and misnamed Bantu tribes, wild hordes that had descended thousands of miles on foot from Central Africa, braving all odds, the women leading the older children, carrying the younger ones on their backs and their loads on their heads, stopping on the way to bear a baby like sheep on the downs, while the men drove and milked the cattle, and battled with wild beasts and with one another. Migration was to a certain extent determined by the need to thin out overcrowded areas and to find pastures for their droves, but it was also an urge in their blood, for they did not stop when occasion presented itself. Some of these migrations lasted for centuries, and to-day when the wanderlust descends upon them, as they cannot quit the land, those in a location often transfer their kraals to another part of it.

The perilous conditions of these migrations, by the way, are responsible for many of their still surviving customs, and are the reason why the men never carry loads or do any housework. This is illustrated by the following example. Not so very long ago, a matter of these last few years, a mistaken young white official new to Central Africa, and with all his ideas in need of adjustment to his surroundings, happened to meet a tribe on the march, the women loaded up, the men herding the cattle. In a fit of virtuous indignation he called on the men authoritatively to relieve the women of their loads, bidding them carry them as they did for a stranger. He had the whole posse of women screaming and raving

NATIONALISM FALLS INTO RUSSO-GERMAN TRAP

round him. "When they do porterage their defence is the affair of the escort," they yelled. "And how will they look after the cattle with loads on their heads?" (He learnt it was a religious taboo for women.) "And who will defend us if we are attacked by raiders?" (There is still a good deal of raiding for slaves and general brigandage going on; much more than supercilious white readers imagine, or would care to hear about.) "Do you want us to be mauled by the lions, you heartless and meddlesome foreigner?" The white official beat an undignified retreat, it is said, a sadder and a wiser man.

No, Africa is not the land for the weak or the unprotected, and much maudlin sentiment is wasted by people who would do better to mind their own business, instead of always thinking they can talk of Africa without knowing anything about it. And probably the weak tribes were on the whole better off in those days as slaves in cruel America than enjoying the doubtful freedom of their own country. The real horror of slavery lay in the fact that white men and women could descend to such beastliness and still be called respectable and civilized.

The higher family sentiments and the noble desire for regular and lasting families through free unions with mates of their own choice are not African characteristics, but were acquired by the slaves through their contact with the white man's civilization. Among the primitive tribes of Africa, where the family is the cardinal pivot on which the entire tribal system revolves, women are mere chattels to be disposed of at the pleasure of the men in whose charge they happen to be at the moment. They can be given in marriage to a man they hate, because he has the bride price ready, while the man they would choose is not in a position to claim them; or they may be forced to replace a childless sister, or repudiated on account of sterility, to drag out the miserable existence of moral outcasts. When widowed, they belong to the dead man's assets and are disposed of by the heir. As a rule native law, in contrast with its care in disposing meticulously of the rights and duties of a mother, disregards utterly her human sentiments and feelings. Therefore the slaves themselves did not expect free choice of a mate, and could not pine for lasting unions until, through contact with white civilization, they had learnt of the existence of both.

But to return to the original subject of the tribes of South Africa. It was not these sturdy races, which had survived the hardships and dangers of the long trek, that would tempt the slave-raiders, for they were fierce and warlike, and the last thing on earth a slave-raider wanted was to fall into their hands. Besides, why go so far? The tribes that were raided for the American market were those of the Central African coast and its hinterland. And their blood relationship with the tribes of the south was after so long an interval very much diluted, while their intercourse had been nil. In the good old days if they had lived anywhere within reach of each other, the warriors of the south would have swept periodically over their land, killing all they did not want and carrying off those they did, and the survivors among them, those who had escaped destruction by flight or hiding, would have stolen out when all was over and roasted the bodies of the slain, dancing round the fire and singing while the succulent meal was being cooked.

In America the negroes were plunged headlong into the midst of white civilization; perhaps rather a rudimentary one, as most Americans would discover if they had to experience a return to it, yet miles above their own. Further, it shattered at one blow all their old traditions and customs, for not even on the big plantations where they were living in large numbers could they keep up cannibalism at all, or to any great extent witch-doctoring. When they were enfranchised and took to free matrimony, it had to be on the footing of monogamy and without any attempt to revive the bride price or any substitution of it. They went to church and to school long before the members of their tribes had ever heard of either, and were complaining of the meagreness of their pay before the revelation of money had reached their ancestral homes. When Duwane arrived among them they had their farms, and even today private land tenure is not admitted by native law; they had an ecclesiastical hierarchy and their Universities, all things beyond the conception of the African mind. However horrid the white man was, his country and his ways they had found good; nevertheless their fury against him was as great as that of the Africans of Africa.

It has been said in an earlier chapter, and is maintained, that Christianity is a disintegrating force in Africa, and that it has on the whole appealed rather to the inferior type of native. However, it has also already been said that some very honest attempts have been made on the part of the natives to follow in the path set by the missionaries. Not very often, it is true, and those who have succeeded in keeping to it are always to be found at the doors of the white man under his direct protection, or living under white conditions in some larger village or town absolutely detached from the obligations of their environment. In America, among the slaves, the better elements became very friendly with their masters, real bonds rose between them, and some slaves revealed a soul as noble and as gentle as those of any white. The best blacks responded to the good in their new surroundings and behaved in a most exemplary manner. But on the whole, even among the blacks of America, heredity

NATIONALISM FALLS INTO RUSSO-GERMAN TRAP

is still so strong that they retain all their original fundamental characteristics; and they refuse to believe that civilization is a radical transformation to be reached only through the modification of fundamentals, not an end to be achieved by waving a magical wand. It must work from the interior towards the exterior, and cannot be assumed like a garment or by investiture with a diploma. It is a sign of inner grace shining through one's actions and feelings because it dominates the soul; it is no gorgeous suit to cover the putridness of a low and beastly mind. There is something intangible and indefinable in it that substitutes one line of reasoning for another, and modifies the rules of behaviour that make for civilization. It comes slowly and painfully, for it is an hereditary intuition that takes generations to assert itself before the transformation of the inner consciousness can be accomplished. Also it is partly habit, an unconscious grouping of thoughts, involuntary reactions of reflexes that must be inborn and cannot be induced by expediency.

The negroes of America do not seem to realize to what extent they owe their advancement to their surroundings, to the daily and hourly contact with the white man, to the impossibility of escaping from the iron discipline of an external code of behaviour that forces them to keep within certain bounds and outside certain others. They

THE SEETHING AFRICAN POT

refuse to appreciate how much they are favoured by an environment offering them the means of materializing some of their most cherished ambitions and a wide scope for their activities. Introspection and self-analysis are not negro traits, and they carefully avoid cultivating them; for if they did they would have to admit how little their fundamental characteristics are changed by all these advantages, and might later conjure up a most unhappy picture of what the negroes of America might revert to if they lived for some time out of the white man's hated influence, with discipline relaxed, and their own untamed natures again in full sway.[1] That they have some men and women of high intellectual standard and business capacity all who know them are ready to grant, but that on the whole their inner evolution is not as far advanced as their external one, owing to the force of their environment, is a truth as evident to dispassionate observers as it is displeasing to them. It has taken the white man thousands of years to evolve his very imperfect personality, and crude subjects projected into his moral atmosphere cannot absorb it.

This truth is established by their failure to maintain their level once these forced creatures return to their natural surroundings. There are

[1] An example of this is Liberia, where the liberated slaves have revived most evils of primitive life, including slavery in its worst form.

NATIONALISM FALLS INTO RUSSO-GERMAN TRAP

innumerable instances of this, of natives ordained in Christian churches in Europe that back in their native land have "reverted to type"; of natives with brilliant medical degrees taken in Europe and America succumbing to the mystic lures of witchcraft; of officers who discard their tunics and cast off their accoutrements to revel wholeheartedly together with their primitive brethren in the untutored life of the kraal.

Very, very recently a young Congolese post-office official disappeared mysteriously from his situation in town. He had been to Europe and had not only attended the higher schools, but had also passed the first course of a university in Belgium. Some time later he was discovered in his native village, happy in resuming his normal life untrammelled by clogging clothing or any other restriction of civilization, assisted by the merry companionship of eleven buxom young wives his earnings had permitted him to collect.

At the time of Duwane's appeal to them, the American negroes had advanced to a stage of civilization that must have appeared highly exalted in the eyes of the African envoys, but as a matter of fact it was very fourth-rate, and they were not sufficiently developed themselves to conduct successfully so grave an undertaking as the redemption of Africa from bondage to the white man.

Dispassionately reviewing at a distance of time

THE SEETHING AFRICAN POT

the progress of black nationalism in Africa and its slow evolution under the management of the negroes of America, it is evident that what they had fostered for years with the illusion of preparing an essentially revolutionary machinery, which they had calculated to perfect by elaborate plans cherished over a long period of strenuous preparation, really amounted to little more than a nebulous groping after some mystical goal. However, considering the immaturity of the American negroes themselves, it is very much to their credit that they succeeded as far as they did in organizing an anti-white campaign in so distant a continent, in obtaining co-ordination of aims between two such antagonistic groups as the Christian and the pagan natives, and in moulding them into one homogeneous mass of seething discontent and virulent hatred throughout the greater part of the African continent from the Equator south, which they kept for years in a continual state of turmoil and festering rebellion.

Still, it got no further than that, and the situation would probably have dragged along in a sequence of local outbreaks for many more years, if it had not been for the unfortunate circumstance of so many natives from various parts of Africa being sent to Europe at the time of the Great War, to fight in the ranks or work in the Labour Corps.

White prestige in the Far East had received a

NATIONALISM FALLS INTO RUSSO-GERMAN TRAP

nasty knock on the head by the Russo-Japanese war, for it destroyed the legend of the white man's invincibility before the coloured races, and the echo of his defeat had reached Africa. There it did not have much more than the effect of sowing another seed of the weed that was to choke out white prestige, for it can hardly be said to have penetrated the melanic consciousness at the time. It was assimilated when the Great War came and the Mother Countries called upon the colonies for help in the face of the disapproval and in defiance of the warnings of experts in native psychology. In the first instance the hitherto sacrosanct respect for the white man's life, that for centuries had been imposed on coloured peoples by the harshest reprisals, was trampled upon by the white man himself when he equipped the coloured peoples with arms and sent them out to slaughter his fellow whites. They, the coloured peoples, asked for nothing better, and the rank, acrid smell of the white man that had so offended their nostrils at home, when mixed with the reek of his gushing blood, became the sweetest perfume they had ever known.

In Europe the African saw too much of the seamy side of the white man's life; of murder, rape, pillage, wholesale pollution, an eroticism as bad as his own, indulged in by men and women shamelessly and openly, with complete impunity. And worst of all, he made the acquaintance of the white-slave traffic, and found it to his taste. White women often fell to his lot free of charge, or for a few shillings he could easily procure one. Too ignorant and too brutal to understand any of the grandeur and nobility in the white man or appreciate his industry and his many achievements, all that appealed to him was just the baseness and the bestiality lurking in his nature, the latent savagery that thousands of years of civilization had striven to eradicate and had at last subdued, until the war revived it. War is a crucible of the nobility of man, and many whites had not borne the test. With secular ambitions relaxed, standards of clean living and clean thought bedraggled in the gory mire of the living hell of trench life, the nobler elements had emerged purified and exalted by the struggle in which the baser sort had reverted to the savagery of primeval man, only deadlier in that he was better equipped to strike. Progress and science at the service of bloodlust and hatred produce a fiercer beast than any untutored native fighting naked with knife and spear. The native, on the other hand, promoted from nakedness to a tidy uniform, from knife and spear to rifle and machine-gun, with a free hand in killing white men, with white women to debauch, was uplifted beyond his wildest dreams and thought himself a very fine fellow indeed. Because they met on the same plane, the degraded white man and the elated black, the black man gloated over the discovery and easily convinced himself even more of the equality of the races.

With such a spiritual preparation, is it surprising that coloured peoples should enthusiastically rush to the banner of Communism as the ideology of destruction and the promise of violence in complete unison with their own tastes? It would be hard to say which side was more eager, whether the coloured people to obtain membership in so beautiful an organization, or the Communist party to admit them to it.

Communism, with a mixed leadership of white and colour, devoted great care to the establishment of a revolutionary press, whether in the vernacular of the country, in the language of the dominant race, or both. Africa was immediately deluged by it, and it is the very plague among primitive peoples, who are so easily excited, so easily deluded, so prone to believe anything that pleases them. Readers incapable of discernment are excessively condoled with in their troubles, flattered with undeserved praise, extolled as ready for undertakings whose import they cannot even realize. Subtle insinuations about the new future and the sacred rights of primitive peoples are freely interspersed with seraphic descriptions of infallible happiness under the new order as soon as it is established, alternating with visions of freedom untrammelled by the odious restrictions of detested aliens.

They are told, and therefore believe, that they are ready to rise and vindicate themselves at any cost against the arrogance of greedy adventurers battening on ill-gotten gains obtained by exploiting the unfortunate natives. And the insidiousness of the trash that is purveyed corrupts still further a taste already depraved, exciting the worst lusts and passions till any nobility in the idea of nationalism is completely smothered by the ghoulish desire for an orgy of massacre.

The pan-negro movement in America counted at this time two large political societies: the National Association for the Advancement of the Coloured Peoples and the Universal Negro Improvement Association. Under their patronage the First World Congress of Coloured Peoples was held in Paris, contemporaneously with the Peace Conference. In answer to their invitation delegates rushed in from the far corners of the earth, in raptures at the opportunity for airing their grievances before so sympathetic an audience, and of strutting about in the limelight of so exceptional a stage. Outsiders looked on with disdain and condescension, highly amused at the spectacle of ethnical immaturity and business incompetence displayed at the meetings.

No sooner was the congress in Paris over than another one was called at Madison Square, New

NATIONALISM FALLS INTO RUSSO-GERMAN TRAP

York, which provided almost a carnival of laughter among the whites as Marcus Garvey, an "intellectual" negro from the Antilles, and one of the principal propounders of pan-negroism, proclaimed himself simultaneously King of the Black Peoples and Provisional President of the Continent of Africa, to the huge delight of the negroes themselves, who were vastly relieved by this great step forward, and felt that things were really beginning to take shape at last.

It was a splendid stroke of policy which Garvey knew could not fail to move the hearts of his people, and he hastened to follow it up by presenting himself before the exulting crowds arrayed in a regal mantle of purple velvet richly embellished with gold. His staff, also, strove to imitate him, adorning themselves in equally fantastic if less gorgeous attire. As a climax he compared himself to Napoleon, a pet weakness of negroes; they do it on the slightest provocation, and are always moved by it very deeply. This is aptly illustrated by the unexpected effect of a comparison made by students of history between the French Emperor and Tchaka, the great Zulu warrior chief. Possibly historians may be right in affirming that his military genius was of the same class as Napoleon Bonaparte's, but there is no doubt that in his lifetime he was one of the most bloodthirsty tyrants even Africa has ever seen, and he never disguised his distrust of missionaries nor his dislike for a religion extremely hampering to a person of his propensity to hack his prisoners to pieces by the hundred, or to push them over a cliff to get rid of them quicker. Yet, when this appreciation was published, his gratified descendants, probably very vague as to what was meant, but dimly conscious of an implied compliment, promptly founded the "Tchaka Zulu Church," blissfully unaware of any incongruity and superbly indifferent to the feelings of that monarch, whose bones probably turned in his grave at the insult.

Making due allowance for the emotionalism of the blacks, Communism grew busy with them wherever they could be found. Africa was overrun with propagandists, black and white, the negro centres in America and Europe were carefully attended to, agents met ships at all the ports to catch black workers (mostly stokers) and students as they landed, shepherding them for instruction to the nearest cell, under Soviet control if not of direct Soviet origin.

In Africa Communism made huge strides by its arguments, its activity, its fulsome adulation of the natives backed by largesse sapiently distributed, easily gaining a hearing from the Bantu tribes eager to listen to useful hints on the art of rebellion and the fascinating trade of contraband in arms.

At a very early date after taking over the

NATIONALISM FALLS INTO RUSSO-GERMAN TRAP

direction of affairs in Africa, the apostles of Bolshevism declared it absurd that the slogan "Africa for the Africans" should be limited to its original significance of a demand for ecclesiastical independence and equality with the whites, and pronounced it an inferior and obsolete programme for black nationalism. They proclaimed that its true purport was "Down with the white man's religion and out with the white man himself from the country." Meanwhile, any little omission in the field of anti-white organization was tactfully rectified as the Ntambwe-Bwanga society among the backward natives of the Congo amply testifies.

Having once tasted the joys of international congresses, the coloured peoples went simply wild about them, and coloured congresses in white countries became the order of the day, at which agitators of all races gave vent to diatribes blasting with infamy the white man and all his institutions. Monumental liars purposefully explained away with a few vitriolic phrases any advantages coloured peoples in Africa and Asia had derived from the white man's rule, plotting and planning ways and means to create disaffection and provoke riots, methodically inflaming hatred and savagery in their immediate hearers, leaving to their press the care of disseminating the venom through the world, and to the agents commissioned to carry out the wishes of the congresses in the various countries allotted to them, the business of explaining the doctrines to those whom the press did not reach or who could not themselves apply notions so fantastic.

This after all has been the avowed intention of Bolshevism everywhere, but in Africa there was in addition the edifying spectacle of the Watchtower apostles preaching wholesale massacre and revolution under the cloak of Christianity.

From the first Communism put its best foot forward in the task of enticing all coloured peoples into its ranks, and by 1925 its reorganization in America was so far advanced that the Soviet considered it high time to take over control into its own hands.

Senator Coty, in his famous articles, gives the whole story of the transaction. He tells how Rietchensky, then chief of the Soviet secret police in New York, opened under orders relations with the negro party with the purpose of forming a left wing under its direct control in the U.S.A. The negotiations were successful, and another branch was started, naturally composed chiefly of workers, that took the name of "The Colored Men's Association." Largely subventioned by the Kremlin the Association did not so much propose operating within the U.S. as raising international questions of black labour in the colonies.

This step immediately split the American negro party whose aim had been the elevation of the negro by means of general education through the schools and universities that were so largely frequented and were giving what they considered such first-rate results that the blacks considered themselves entitled thereby to equality with the whites, and resented any denial of this claim. To the minds of the blacks the proved value of a few exceptions was held to cover the inferiority of the masses, the honesty and soundness of the hundreds to excuse the barbarity and backwardness of the millions, and they could not see any other explanation of the white man's attitude than congenital perversity and racial prejudice. On the subject of this much ill-applied word volumes might be written, for the negroes are just as badly tarred with the same brush, and are blinded by it to the benefits received from the white man's civilization and aid; and if they could overcome their racial antagonism towards the white man and make up their minds to accept his teachings in a better spirit and strive to follow painfully in his footsteps for a couple of centuries, renouncing their hatred for him and reducing their envy of him, they would probably reap a much higher benefit and be all-round happier than they are or can be in their present ugly mood. In their conceit of their success, they forget, or choose to disremember, how much they owe to the white man, and while still stumbling and slipping in their efforts to catch up with him on a path of his hewing, they go to the length of ungrate-

THE SEETHING AFRICAN POT

fully denying it as his work. Instead of thanking him for kindly consenting to let them tread it without demanding of them that they should first train in the art of roadmaking, and for pointing out to them how best to set their feet, they think it their prerogative to push him off it, and demand that he reduce his gait to the measure of their own faltering pace, while trying themselves to push into the front ranks, dreaming of presently supplanting him in laying down the track.

Often in their talk of equality there is more than a hint that they consider themselves in an unexplained way his superior, just as they shamelessly try to show that the wealth of Africa has gone wholly into his pockets, or that without black labour the white man could not get on in the land.

The tactics pursued by Communism among the negroes of America closely resembled those employed by the American negro leaders of Ethiopianism among the primitive tribes of Africa. And just as the American negroes led their backward brethren by the nose, so they in their turn became the tools and dupes of men so far cleverer than they as to allow the negroes to believe themselves their equals and to play them with this bait at their pleasure.

The initial step was to plash them from the existing organizations and to gain complete control of their actions. Therefore the earlier leaders had to be held up to ridicule and vilification, while spurious adulation did the rest. This combination succeeded among the black as excellently as it succeeded among the white proletariat. The confirmation of what has been said can be found in George Padmore's *Life and Struggles of Negro Toilers*. As he is a cherished secretary of communistic organizations his authority is most reliable and unimpeachable, especially as his book was officially published in 1931 by the Red International Labour Union. This book makes most interesting reading for it shows the arguments by which the proletariat of all colours is excited and instigated to rebellion. It urges the negro workers not to allow themselves to be misled by what Padmore calls the "left" phrases of the American negro petty bourgeoisie reformists who, in his opinion, are merely office seekers and demagogues at the service of the ruling classes with the intent to distract the attention of the negroes from their special aspirations.

Writing of Garveyism, he calls it a dangerous ideology to be strongly resisted because of its ambition to establish a negro Kingdom, a proposal he considers damaging the mass negro struggle for freedom from American Imperialism. He declares the movement in itself as bankrupt, and regrets that its empty ideology still appeals to so many blacks; and he warns them that by still adhering to it they play up to the interests of black capitalists, who would be the people to profit by a Negro Republic in Africa as it would allow them to exploit the black proletariats without fear of white competition. For Padmore the danger of Garveyism lies in its class content as very deceiving to the masses, which must instead be induced to persevere on the path leading to fusion with the class-conscious white workers of all imperialistic countries, besides aiming at an alliance with the coloured proletariats of Asiatic countries and South America, since only an organization millions strong can hope to effectually succeed in ending world imperialism.

Padmore explains the racial outbreaks in America very characteristically as the work of business and professional men, whom he accuses of making "periodical raids upon the black countryside." According to him, these business and professional men have formed into bands for this purpose, and he indicates especially the Ku Klux Klan, the American Legion, the Blackshirts and the Caucasian Crusaders as the bodies maintained by the bourgeoisie and the reactionary middle-class elements for the express purpose of burning alive black men, women and children, and of pillaging their homes. Poisoning of drinking wells, carrying off of livestock belonging to the victims form other minor items of racial antagonism, so that, as Mr. Padmore declares, "any negro in America is absolutely at the mercy of every fiendish mob incited by the white landlords and capitalists."

It sounds rather a weird way of putting it, but accuracy is not an essential to propaganda. The negroes have to be warmed up somehow, and this is probably as good a method as any other. Mr. Padmore's justification for this ferocity lies in the fact that the bourgeoisie and landlords belong to the class of former slaveowners and therefore have a congenital urge for committing all sorts of brutalities against a race they consider not as human beings but as mere chattels. Torture is represented as a sort of pastime of the ex-slaveowners. The ruling classes are accused of maintaining "a reign of fascist terrorism throughout the state apparatus (court, police, militia), as well as the Church." To an outsider all this seems scarcely more than a disjointed jargon, a hopeless medley of conflicting terms and irrational assertions, but the effect on excited crowds, those crowds that yell at the bare mention of certain words without even waiting to hear their purport, must be enormous.

Mr. Padmore's review of events in Africa is also extremely interesting. First he accuses the British Imperialists of deliberately causing unrest to create situations requiring military intervention for subduing revolts which he later tells us are instigated by a movement he declares is prevalent in East Africa due to the activities of the East

African Association. This he openly qualifies as a revolutionary movement on an organized scale inspired by the Indian revolutionary movement and transported to East Africa by the innumerable Indian revolutionaries residing in Africa to whom he tenders his thanks. Praising what he calls the tremendous proportions of the movement to which he attributes the merit of organizing the frequent strikes and clashes of various sorts that have disturbed Kenya, Uganda, and Tanganyika during these last years, he dedicates a special pæan to the Harry Thuku revolt that gave serious trouble in the Kikuyo province. He omits, however, to inform his readers who Harry Thuku was or what he revolted against, but describes him as a fearless fighter placing himself at the head of a mixed band of young men and women who visited all the villages stirring up the whole country. He explicitly says that Harry Thuku won the universal admiration of all the blacks and "especially of the children who had been forced out of school on purpose to work on the farms." One can easily picture the delight of the dear little pickaninnies and how they must have enjoyed the lark. Unfortunately Thuku's instigation led to a general strike and riots where, Padmore says, machine-guns were used and 150 people lost their lives while many more were wounded. Instead, when he affirms that Harry Thuku's following was so great and

NATIONALISM FALLS INTO RUSSO-GERMAN TRAP

the lack of faith among the soldiers sent out to arrest him too evident for the authorities "daring" to arrest the instigator of the trouble, he discloses again the intention to mislead his readers, for one cannot with any stretch of imagination credit the local government with hesitating to arrest a native rebel for fear of his mass following. Deserving of note, rather, is the insinuation of lack of faith among the soldiery, for this is a topic that is going to crop up again later.

Concerning Basutoland Padmore tells of a native revolutionary organization called Lakhola-Baffo, affiliated to the League Against Imperialism, and of bloody revolts that have recently broken out and been suppressed by air bombing. That a few individual Basuto may belong to such an association, especially outside their own land, their well-known love of secret societies renders quite possible, though not equally probable, but as to the riots and air-bombing of native villages, anybody with the slightest acquaintance with the law-abiding natives of the three Protectorates knows how intensely they long for British protection, how they cling to it in virtue of their covenants with Britain and how careful the chiefs are to avoid any act that might be interpreted as the expression of a wish for a change in administration.

Padmore boasts that the rebellion in Nigeria in 1929 as well as several outbreaks in the Union of South Africa are the outcome of communistic activity. He lays great stress on the revolts of 1924 and 1928 in the French Congo, and the manner in which the facts are presented and interpreted deserves particular attention.

First of all he expresses his satisfaction that the rebellion was able to hold out for four months during which mines and bridges were blown up, and a good deal of property destroyed. He does not give the figures of dead or injured during the conflicts but accuses the government of very sharp reprisals against the native population after the sedition was quelled whereby, in his estimation, more people lost their lives than during the actual rebellion. He affirms that natives were shot on the mere suspicion of having participated in the riots, and that old men and women were publicly whipped in punishment for their own misdeeds or as an example to the population in general, an example that he is proud to say was not taken to heart, for fresh riots broke out again in April 1930.

Kibango's revolt Padmore classifies as one of the most formidable anti-imperialistic movements in Central Africa. It was organized by the native carpenter Kibango when he discovered that his missionary teachers were the tools of the imperialists. As a result, Kibango hastened to induce his black brethren to quit all missions and to renounce the white man's teaching and religion, and

NATIONALISM FALLS INTO RUSSO-GERMAN TRAP

founded a separate native church. However, even Padmore admits that the movement very soon changed from a religious to a political one, reinforced by the efforts of alien native students from British and West African territories. This eventually led to grave disturbances, resulting in Kibango's arrest, court-martial and sentence of death, while other ringleaders were condemned to various terms of imprisonment. Padmore also mentions a girl called Mandami who was condemned to two years' imprisonment and was described by the prosecution at the trial as the most revolutionary woman in the Congo. One cannot help wondering whether Mandami really was her name, or whether more probably she may have been the wife of a Ntambwe Mwine, preferring to declare a fancy title rather than her own name.

Padmore contends that the sentences irritated the natives to such an extent that strikes and riots of protest broke out all over the colony, and so completely arrested the economic life that the exasperated Europeans demanded the public execution of Kibango, a demand that was countered by a threat from the enraged blacks to set on and exterminate the whites. This situation would have been so serious that not only Kibango's sentence was commuted into imprisonment for life, but some of his companions had theirs completely remitted. A certain amount of order appears to have been established after this compromise, but

Padmore proclaims the movement to be still flourishing, "notably among the younger generation who are breaking away from tribal influences thanks to their proletarianism and increased class-consciousness."

When reviewing Ruanda and Urundi George Padmore enlightens us also on the connection between the Nabingi and the communist party although he never mentions the name of the society. The unrest ending in conflict in those regions he ascribed to the traditional Belgian policy of depriving the natives of their land in order to give it to white speculators, in consequence of which famine spread over the land, culminating in grave riots in 1929, as the Belgian authorities denied any relief to the starving population and the neighbouring British deliberately forebade any food being sent to them. Driven to exasperation the unfortunate natives of Belgian Ruanda broke out of control, the disaffection quickly spreading to British territory. The rebellion seems to have had one leader for both districts, and it was a woman, vaguely described as the daughter of the king of Ruanda. At a place given as Gatsolon, native chiefs known to be friendly, or at least submissive to white rule, were murdered, besides Belgian officials and soldiers. The Belgian colonial government rushed troops to the scene, but not for some time was order re-established. The defeated ringleaders fled towards Uganda pursued

NATIONALISM FALLS INTO RUSSO-GERMAN TRAP

by the Belgians, but when they reached British territory they were seized and delivered into the hands of the Belgians. At this point Padmore says that a brother of the king of Ruanda was among the prisoners, and that he suffered the extreme penalty in company with more than a thousand companions. As there is confusion as to the sex of the leader, who first was described as a sister, and then as a brother of the king of Ruanda, there may be also a slight error in the number of prisoners shot. Still it is practically certain that the leader was a near relation of the king of Ruanda as it coincides with information from all other sources. Padmore states that a mixed Anglo-Belgian force was installed at Kiforte to prevent further troubles, but brags that in spite of all superficial discouragement, the black agitation has in reality received a tremendous impetus from the rebellion.

Senator Coty devoted as great an attention to the World Congress held at Moscow in July and August 1928 as if he had been the most rampageous of Reds. On this subject he writes:

"It was attended by delegates from all the world, and when the subject of propaganda in Africa came up for discussion, members were informed that penetration among its black population though still on the threshold, was advancing considerably and would prosper further provided the way was found to lay a practical foundation on which to rest it, and passwords sufficiently simple for use even by the most ignorant negroes were coined. On August 1 a special meeting was called with instructions definitely to organize propaganda among the negro proletariat, and the following committee was elected among the negro delegates present :

American negroes	2 delegates	Angola	1 delegate
Guadaloupe	1 ,,	Moçambique	1 ,,
Martinique	1 ,,	Congo (French and Belge)	1 ,,
Haiti	1 ,,	Senegal and Soudan	1 ,,
Cuba	1 ,,	Liberia	1 ,,
Union of S. Africa	1 ,,	British E.A.	1 ,,

"Of these thirteen delegates all, except the six representatives of the U.S.A. and the Antilles, were American negroes settled in Africa for the purpose of anti-white propaganda.

"A motion was then passed affirming the solidarity of all the negroes of all the world in the aim of freeing Africa, the Mother Country of the whole black race. There still remained to fix the financial base of the new organization, for although the American negroes were yet to man it, it was considered incumbent on the Soviets to stand the expense. A first contribution of 200,000 roubles was in fact offered on the spot, but much more must have been paid out later."

The congress adjourned on the motion of the Angola delegate, who announced with a cannibalistic guffaw that when the hour struck for its liberation, the African proletariat would know how to avenge itself upon white capitalism

NATIONALISM FALLS INTO RUSSO-GERMAN TRAP

and white colonization in a manner never to be forgotten.

"It is evident," was Coty's comment on the proceedings of the congress, "that the American instructors and animators of their backward African brethren head straight for actual warfare against the European conqueror. The mere conception of an Africa united and independent presupposes the violent crumbling of colonial domination equally, whether British, French or Portuguese, etc., and it ought to have been in itself sufficient to cause a strict watch to be set on all forms of American Negro infiltration into Africa; especially that of black missionaries, of whom there have been an abnormal increase during the last ten years."

The advice was not accepted, and Coty was ranked among the alarmists, those scaremongers who heard the rumblings of the approaching storm. Yet communist propaganda among the coloured peoples, the black especially, was being carried on very actively through the whole of France, with its centre in Paris itself. No clearer details of it could be found than Coty's history of it.

"In 1924 the Ligue Universelle pour la Défence de la Race Noire was founded in Paris, but did not last long owing to misadventures caused by the frailty of its president, who had succeeded in passing cheques to the amount of 400,000 francs before the public discovered that they were worthless. However, Moscow saw to it that so valuable an organization should not remain too long inactive, and on July 4th, 1926, at the Salle des Hautes Etudes Sociales, Rue de la Sorbonne, it was revived under the name of Comité de Défence de la Race Nègre. The following telegram sent by its board at its opening session is so clear that no comment is necessary:

"Au Comité Exécutif Elargi de L'Internationale Communiste Moscou.

"Portons a votre connaissance élection de Lenin Présidence Honoraire perpetuelle Comité. Saluons fraternellement ouverture séance, examen situation mondiale. Attirons généreuse attention sur monde nègre travailleur. Faisons voeux travail commun pour réaliser sincère fraternité universelle.

"Pour le Comité de la Race Nègre
"le sécrétaire général
"J. GOTHON LUNIOU.

"For the uninitiated," as Coty explains, "the avowed intentions of the league were to help coloured people materially and in their studies, and it opened a 'home' for newly-arrived negroes without means or friends. In reality it masked its real identity, that of a branch of the Ligue contre l'Impérialism et l'Oppression Colonial created by the Third International, that openly aims at 'co-ordinating throughout the whole world all revolutionary movements directed against occidental and imperialistic domination.'"

Padmore, our previous source of information, declares that the initiative of drawing the negro workers into the world-wide communistic organization lies with the class-conscious white workers, who must also learn to make place for the negroes

NATIONALISM FALLS INTO RUSSO-GERMAN TRAP

in the leadership and direction of the proletariat mass agitations. The blacks must be encouraged to become more active in the revolution of the world proletariat, and the necessity for all, white and black, to beware of the imperialist's intention to use the black proletariat in the colonies to lower still further the already deplorable condition of the white workers, is urgent. After expressing the conviction that the territorial aspirations of rival imperialistic nations will inevitably lead to another war, Padmore explains that it is in preparation for this emergency that black armies are being trained and formed. According to him, in war time they will be used for the curious dual purpose of serving as shock troops and as reserve, and in time of peace for suppressing future rebellions in Europe on the day when white troops formed of white proletarians are expected to refuse to obey the commands of their bourgeois officers when ordered to fire on their massed revolutionary brethren. France, especially, is attacked on the grounds that she is heading the imperialists in their anti-Soviet campaign, for her use of black troops for the suppression of strikes in France, and for sending them to her Asiatic colonies.

Anti-white propaganda among colonial troops of all nations was the next step and was undertaken with the whole-hearted earnestness that characterizes these activities. Natives were to be dissuaded from enlisting, those already under

THE SEETHING AFRICAN POT

arms had to be persuaded that fighting for the white man was against their personal and racial interests; by any and every argument they had to be scared off and repelled. The queer reasoning of the natives is illustrated by the conflicting and contradictory arguments laid before them, all obtaining equally their unqualified approval.

George Padmore solemnly assures his readers that the unfortunate negroes of the U.S.A. are obliged to pass their summers in the military training-camps on pain of being dismissed their jobs. This is not true, but it is effective on paper, and natives are notoriously gullible; besides, this lie impressed both the natives of all countries and the white proletariat of all the world.

For the South African natives the persistent refusal of admittance into any branch of the army has always been a cause of grief and humiliation. They offered to fight for the British during the Boer War, but were repulsed. They volunteered individually, and some of the biggest chiefs offered whole battalions during the European War to fight in Africa or in Europe, and all they obtained was work in the Labour Corps. They are only accepted in the Union in the Native Police and in the Offices of the Native Administration. When some years ago the Government of the Union announced the intention of providing for the defence of the country the outcome was awaited with breathless interest. One can imagine

NATIONALISM FALLS INTO RUSSO-GERMAN TRAP

the disappointment of the natives when the law was passed in 1927, making military training compulsory for all males between the ages of 18 and 50 provided they were of all-white descent. George Padmore does not fail to impress upon his readers that this measure was taken by the white bourgeoisie because they were afraid to arm the natives, as all chance of white domination lies in having one section of the population armed and the other unarmed. Padmore specifies that this is a necessary precaution to enable fascist mobs to swoop down safely on the residential quarters of the defenceless natives who are thus completely at their mercy.

They are hard to please, these leaders, and apparently cannot quite make up their minds which is worse, to be called to, or to be forbidden, military service, and not to make any mistake they commiserate with negroes for whatever comes their way.

When one recalls to mind that for a great many primitive tribes men exist primarily for the purpose of war as women for that of procreation, it is apodeictic that some great force must be at work to deter men from spontaneously embracing a career so consistent with their tastes and their traditions, and that some subtle argument or prize must be dangled before their eyes so utterly irresistible as to smother their savage warrior instincts, to cause them to renounce the ambition of sporting a natty uniform, and to forego the delight of handling firearms.

Propaganda among the soldiery took the form of furnishing cooked statistics of tuberculosis, syphilis and other diseases they were told they would contract inevitably in service, but would escape if they remained at home, and of exaggerated reports on the death-rate of the troops. They were scared with false news of rebellions in their native areas, ruthlessly suppressed at high cost of life. Discontent on account of food, leave, or any other incidents of normal military life was artfully insinuated, and once instilled was magnified into provocation for strikes. The consequences speedily appeared, and dissatisfaction, grumblings and general restiveness superseded the former order and discipline among the ranks. Mutinies among French, British and Dutch troops, and rioting in India were much boasted of shortly afterwards at other congresses, as the merited rewards of their labours.

As Padmore puts it, in 1924, out of 126,000 eligibles, 17,000 Senegalese were "bons absents" when called up for military service. He further affirms that martial law had to be applied to enforce recruitment, and that the general native attitude towards military service had, since the war, entered into an acute stage, not only as a matter of principle, but also because of the bad treatment they received while under arms. Padmore attributes the rebellion of 1928 in French Equatorial Africa, that lasted quite a time, to the natives' opposition to militarism.

Over the home natives of Central and South Africa Communism really gained a hold when the economic stalemate paralysed all forms of local production, for its propaganda exploited inexhaustibly the preponderant topic of unemployment as the one lever to which even the most ignorant masses unfailingly responded. It was a desolation that hung heavily over the land, bringing want and despair into their humble homes. Primitive people cannot be expected to grasp the complicated mechanism of modern trade with its exchanges, its laws of supply and demand, its political limitations and quotas, or the economic repercussions of the oscillations of European fashions in dress, the very existence of which they ignore.

With their arrival the strangers they detested had shattered the normal course of their lives, dragging them from their homes, compelling them to a labour they neither wished for nor saw the sense of. To gratify their greed they had impressed the unwilling natives, and the pain of their displeasure when they met resistance was cruel. The natives told themselves that they bent before the storm because they were helpless to resist it, and they hypnotized themselves by repetition into a fictitious belief that all they longed for was a return to the good old days before the scourge of work had reached their land.

However intensely they resented having to work, or kicked against the injustice of having to pay taxes for administrative improvements they had not asked for, yet they had had their compensations in the many advantages that had accrued to them, in the fun of travelling, the riches they acquired, and ultimately, to their own astonishment, they had even found pleasure in learning to work, and felt pride in their progress.

When the slump came and industrial life in Africa came to a dead stop, with mines closing down, factories at a standstill, and failures all over the land, the natives were first dumbfounded, then incredulous, and finally suspicious. With all output arrested the natives, discovering that nobody asked them any more to go and work, started out on their own account to try and find it, only to be repulsed at every corner and sent home by the authorities. Soon the white men who could afford to do so abandoned the country that had denied them livelihood, as if her soil had become sterile, leaving the natives astounded that what before had been deemed so precious should now be despised as worthless. The crowning injury came when they were turned out of their jobs, that very manual labour which the lordly whites in Africa had decreed derogatory to their own dignity and for which they had paid the natives paltry sums, to make place for the white unemployed, to give them a chance of livelihood at work their tender unaccustomed hands could not do, but for which they were paid at least four times as much as the black, in honour of their colour. Nobody seemed to care what became of the natives, bereft of their means of livelihood; they were cast aside and forgotten till the day for paying their taxes came round, and these were demanded of them in the hard cash they no longer had the means of earning. As they had been reproved and admonished for complaining when called upon to work, now they were reproved and admonished to retire quietly to their distant homes and gracefully resume the interrupted primitiveness of their tribal life. They were not expected to complain, or to murmur at the Protean treatment; like automatons they had been wont to answer to a signal and come out, now let them obey this other signal and go back. The tax collector would visit them at their homes. Away!

They went, with murmurings and mutterings —to listen to the Bolshevist propagandist and his enticements, and take his dross for gold. He came along and explained the situation in terms the natives, however primitive, could grasp. It was a case of deliberate malice and spite on the white man's part. He no longer intended the natives to work for fear of their progress and of their increasing civilization. The white man, he as-

THE SEETHING AFRICAN POT

sured his hearers, had made his huge pile and did not mean to resume business as long as his ill-gotten gains lasted, hoping meanwhile to see the natives die out and so to be rid of them.

Again we learn directly from Mr. Padmore's pen the alluring arguments that trumpeted the new faith to the unhappy Bantu tribes. They were told by the Communists that whereas the capitalistic world was reduced to the worst straits the Soviet Union alone was the land of riches and general emancipation. It had abolished all forms of suppression, had renounced exploitation of the working classes, and extended to the proletariat of all the world its leadership for their revolutionary aspirations, and the overthrow of capitalistic systems. He proclaimed the Soviet Union the "fortress of revolutionary workers."

The natives could not understand such flowery language and did not care about Russia. It is so far away and has no intercourse with Africa. But they pricked up their ears at the phrases that concerned them and hurled themselves pell-mell into the arms of an organization that spoke so straight to their embittered hearts.

George Padmore can be again usefully consulted, for in his smug satisfaction at the success of communist strategy and inspiration he praises the negroes for their awakening and for assuming the counter-offensive against capitalistic exploitation. He declares that by their activity at The

NATIONALISM FALLS INTO RUSSO-GERMAN TRAP

First International Congress of Negro Workers attended by delegates representing the negroes of Africa, South America, West Indies and U.S.A., the negro masses had manifested clearly their advancement in conscious effort towards emancipation. He congratulates these delegates for justifying the confidence reposed in them by not limiting their attentions to local questions alone, but by discussing the general international problems of black proletarianism and racial legislation in Africa.

Senator Coty had a good deal to say on the subject of this conference for, being an alarmist, he had the insight to understand at once where it would lead. It had been planned to meet in London on the first of July, but very unexpectedly British public opinion, weighted by pressure from the Union of South Africa, suddenly reacted, and permission to hold the conference in London was refused. This proved a serious setback at the last moment, and caused disorder in the ranks, so that, curiously enough, it deterred several members from joining when, after frantic search for hospitality, the congress met at Hamburg at the end of the next month. The attendance at Hamburg was much smaller than had been announced for the London venue. But representation was sufficiently widespread to guarantee profitable results, as it contained delegates from all parts of the world, including those from the Far East.

"The conference shall prepare a programme of revolutionary activity for the negroes, with the object of creating an international organization of strife for conducting a unified and organized war against imperialistic oppression. The conference shall decide what measures shall be taken in view of a concerted action of the negro labour masses, and shall create stable relations between the various organizations."

After quoting this, Senator Coty remarks that it

"is perhaps well to specify that the congress was to be attended by representatives of Russian, Indian, Chinese and Japanese communism to ensure a liaison between the communist revolutions of all the world. Its activities were not meant to be restricted to negro emancipation.

"The congress met in Hamburg, a town eminently suited to the purpose of according great facilities to travellers arriving by the German shipping lines, and further for sending off to all parts of the world inflammatory material and seditious propaganda.

"The normal flow of discussion was interrupted by an invitation to transfer the congress to Moscow, but for some inexplicable reason only a select party of twenty-five members accepted the honour.[1] Again the Far Eastern delegates were well in evidence.

"Zeal, however, made up for all numerical deficiencies, and at the meetings held in Moscow two cardinal

[1] Possibly there were qualms in confronting the rampancy of Bolshevism in its fortress home and a fear of adding to a menology they all professed to admire, but scarcely aspired to enter.

NATIONALISM FALLS INTO RUSSO-GERMAN TRAP

decisions were reached. (1) A committee was installed at the Kremlin centralizing all revolutionary propaganda among black peoples. (2) The order was given to provoke the rising of black troops in the service of colonial powers."

On the return to Hamburg of the Moscow delegation, the congress met in full session again, and further resolutions of vital importance were passed, whose purport it is hardly conceivable that the incompetent negroes could understand. As Coty writes:

"A Russo-German secretariat was nominated, destined to foment revolution in French, British and Portuguese colonies. As a matter of fact this secretariat had been functioning discreetly in the background for some time past under the direction of the German communist leader Muesenberg, an expert in colonial questions. Now it will be largely developed, not only thanks to the financial support of Moscow, to whom the negro question is as important as the yellow, but also thanks to the concurrence of the German government.

"The German-Sovietic union, besides being of advantage to the Soviets, serves also the general political interests of Germany, who, not having any more colonies and wishing at least to recover those she has lost, has all the interest to sap the basis of the colonial power of Britain and France. The black agents recruited by Moscow are destined effectually to prepare the way for the resurrection of German domination."

THE SEETHING AFRICAN POT

It is not difficult to visualize the cheering and the thumping that must have greeted these momentous decisions, or to include in the mental picture a vision of the disipient negro delegates hullaballooing with the most riotous, their woolly pates in the clouds, quivering with pride and overwhelmed by the importance of casting their votes at such epoch-making meetings. Intoxicated by high-sounding phrases and the blandishments lavished on them, mesmerized by the flagitious cunning of the Moscow dictators, joyously and weetlessly they undersigned their submission to the white man's will and their readiness to serve his ends. Cloyed by the sticky mellifluous caresses of the Muscovites, in the space of a week the besotted negro delegates had unconsciously foresworn their racial prejudices and renounced the magnetic vision of their victorious emancipation from the white man's thraldom that for forty years of strife had been their patriotic ideal. Prevented by their immaturity from discerning that henceforth at best their agitation could only induce a change of masters, they did not realize that their star of independence had set for ever.

Moscow had twitched the reins of revolt from their incompetent fingers; Hamburg sounded the death-knell of African nationalism. The Russo-German secretariat has since set the fuse for African revolt, the cat's-paw for her own ends.

V ETHIOPIA A PAWN IN THE GAME

Having skilfully induced the deluded blacks voluntarily to resign the direction of their affairs into the hands of the white man and to be proud of placing themselves at the disposal of German aspirations, the Russo-German secretariat, under the presidency of a colonial expert masquerading as a communist leader, lost no time in concentrating with deadly earnestness on the state of affairs in Africa, with the object of preparing a general revolt and of engineering it so that it should overthrow the present distribution of colonies while simultaneously furnishing Germany with some for herself.

From the moment that the treaty of Versailles had been signed Germany had declared that she could not be expected to accept it as definite, and she certainly began intriguing in Africa before the ink on the parchment was dry. One of her first steps had been to insinuate among the natives of Tanganyika and ex-German West Africa the notion that they had been happier and better treated under German rule than they were under mandate, and though it is certainly not the truth, and would never have occurred to the natives themselves, it may even come to prevail through the sapient art and the unsparing efforts by which it is being instilled into them.

A careful examination of the situation showed clearly that, however deeply the native tribes were subverted against their present rulers, Communism in the abstract was not sufficiently strong to dominate them and therefore there yet persisted the necessity for an African ideal round which a general and persevering rebellion could be expected to muster. Most of the tribes were reported as being more or less ready to rise with a spurt, on a local issue that could be pushed to an extreme at will, but such a rising would collapse and die out as the hundreds of preceding ones had done without contributing materially to so vast a scheme as that of the Germans. The complaint made at the congresses that the negroes were insufficiently developed and had still nationalistic tendencies received the attention it deserved, for it is not only perfectly correct, but it portrays a condition of things that will continue. Any colonial expert knows that the Africans have joined Communism wholly for its promises of a general massacre of the whites and the seizure of all their wealth and belongings, relying on the understanding that upon this eventuality the white man's rule will end forever, and native independence be recovered; that nobody will work any more, that there will be no more taxes to pay, and that everybody will be rich and happy, well dressed and civilized, and have all they want for nothing. It is waste of breath to try to tell them something of the conditions of Russia, to explain to them how hard everybody has to work there, and that after all is said and done, production under Soviet rule is for the state and not for the worker, or to suggest that Liberia, the black republic, is not the Garden of Eden they imagine. They are deaf to this, and knowingly reply that the speaker is evidently not a Communist or he would be better informed. They are fully and deeply convinced that once the country was rid of white rule, and they could get a black communism going, all their troubles would be at an end.

In the circumstances it is plain to whomsoever has eyes to see, that a rebellion to be general and enduring has to rally round a great and beloved chief like Mkawa or be enforced by a fighter and a living terror imposing his will like Bichubirenga. But leaders of this calibre are born and cannot be made to order; the very handling of native aspirations by alien, mercenary Communists, black and white, at the orders of a foreign organization utilizing them for its own ends, breaks the magic spell of pure patriotism and taints the atmosphere that produces moral giants and heroes. Though the spirit of revolution is more widespread than it used to be, years of subservience to foreigners have destroyed its spontaneous, indomitable glamour and appeal, together with its disinterested virility. The Nabingi are still powerful in their district, but this is considerably reduced in area and there is no shadow of doubt that the prestige of their paramount chief is weakened, and his authority much less than in the days when the name of N'Toki M'bili or one of his apostles was sufficient to paralyse with terror the most powerful and the most dauntless in the land.

Xenophobia in Africa had attained its greatest moral height while the whole fabric had rested on the catchword of Ethiopia, the Great African Mother, a metaphor that had never consolidated into reality, for even in her best days of popularity she had never been more than a lodestar. None of the Bantu tribes that had invoked her name had actually expected at any moment to be annexed by that unknown and distant country, nor had Ethiopia herself up to then shown any desire to set about such a venture. This being the case, the question arose, by virtue of what secret attribute had this mysterious ideal established such an ascendancy over millions of ignorant and primitive peoples that they should enshrine it in their hearts, live up to it, and die for it? And afterwards, what had caused its decline? The answers are not far to seek.

ETHIOPIA A PAWN IN THE GAME

The criticism that has been made of the black man's assumption, or lack of assumption, of white civilization now applies inversely to black nationalism in Africa, for this was a movement that originated in the very core of the negroes and worked outwards towards the masses. In spite of the regrettable fact that many of its adherents were actuated by selfish motives of ambition and self-aggrandizement, the leaders were all local people and had at least found their reward in the gratifications of power; they had never been swayed by the expediency of mercenary retribution.

Ethiopianism with all its defects, in spite of its unfortunate lure for opportunists and its weakness for swelling its ranks with undesirables and inferior elements, had been the spontaneous growth of black nationalism once this sentiment had been roused, and the urge for self-expression and the hope of self-government had been induced in the natives of Africa. Bishop Turner uttered an incontrovertible truth when he described the black man as being "still asleep," and he gave an irresistible signal when he sounded his trumpet to call on the African to "awake and rise."

But since the advent of socialism among the American negroes and the dawn of the ecstatic days of spasmodic international congresses, the Ethiopian ideal had petered out before the new glory of Marcus Garvey as Sovereign of all the Blacks, and Provincial President of Africa, the Black Napoleon orating in his regal mantle of purple and gold, peacocking on platforms and laying himself out to impress the world with his genius and up-to-date proficiency.

Alas for Marcus! His traditions were too strong for him, his congenital asthenia too overpowering to be held in abeyance by his kingship, his unregeneracy too pronounced to be covered by his regal mantle of purple velvet and gold. The story can best be left to George Padmore's eloquent pen, for he is very hard on Garvey, calling him more than a dishonest pedagogue, accusing him of exploiting the struggles of the negroes against imperialistic oppression for his own ends, and of hampering the development of their movement for several years. Padmore roundly qualifies Garvey's "dishonesty and fraudulent business schemes, such as the Black Star Line," by means of which he swindled his black brethren of their hard-earned gains for a huge sum, for which he was later imprisoned, and having served his time was deported back to his native land of Jamaica. Yet he seems worried about the amount of influence this black man still exerts over his American and European confrères.

Garvey's popularity, at one time immense, inevitably suffered a severe eclipse in consequence of his misadventure, although he managed to get

ETHIOPIA A PAWN IN THE GAME

something of a party together again when he emerged from his enforced retirement. Nevertheless, his popularity was among his confrères of America and Europe rather than those of Africa. Indeed, it is very doubtful if the mass of primitive natives in Africa ever heard of him at all, or, having heard of him, ever realized what he was meant to represent. At the most he may have been a vague name, a sort of distant witch-doctor performing among the white people his incantations to encompass their destruction, or the materialized spirit of some ancestor living among the enemy in order to be able to send his people reliable messages as a guidance for their conduct. They could never have visualized a general African republic or have contemplated a King in the flesh whom nobody had ever seen, whose descent nobody knew and who had never led a revolt. Primitives demand something more real, substantial and tangible; they cannot be content with vague and immaterial chiefs on earth.

Communism recognized its defeat in Africa and attempted to retrieve its position when it named the committee of thirteen members in 1928, a committee that failed signally in its object, inasmuch as it was unable to suggest the measures to win over the reluctant masses and secure their allegiance to the party. The exegesis of this is to be found in the R.I.L.U.; in its number for

November 1932 it publishes a report of the situation in Africa from which the following passage is quoted:

"The many serious mistakes committed by the African Federation of Trade Unions in its today activities in almost complete isolation from the masses in the basic industries are due to the fact that our members do not know how to approach the masses, or how to carry on the struggle for . . ."

There is this much to be said for the Communists, that they are franker and admit their failures more readily and explicitly than other organizations, disdaining to gloss them over.

Of the "many serious mistakes" the principal ones may be scheduled in a very few comprehensive headings.

(1) An absolute disregard of the human element in native discontent. The natives are ready to support any wild scheme that offers a chance for betterment for them, but are not to be carried away by vacuous preachings of empty theoretical dogmatism.

(2) Unmitigated ignorance on the part of its agents, whether white men or alien, detribalized negroes, of the attachment of the natives to their ancestral customs and traditions, which they neglected when they were not rudely trampling them underfoot.

(3) The assumption that the roaring welcome

ETHIOPIA A PAWN IN THE GAME

accorded to them by the few tens of thousands of workers in direct contact with the white man reflected the outlook and sentiments of the millions that were out of reach of disintegrating examples and subversive propaganda, and could counteract the direct pressure of their original environment, with its stern and uncompromising enforcement of discipline.

Ethiopianism was an unadulterated African product and followed the beaten track in its methods of persuasion of the masses; it found its leaders through the traditional media, whereas Communism, an alien thought introduced by foreign and mercenary agents, ignorant and heedless of Bantu psychology, carried no message to the bulk of the population living its primitive life out in the wilds.

Like the missionaries before them, Communist agents were misled by the apparent pliability of the natives, their easy psittacism, their superficial amenability hiding an ingrained aversion to and suspicion of change. And the new doctrine, in spite of its dazzling promises which appealed in moments of exasperation and hardship, proved, when examined in the retirement of village gatherings and analysed in discussion, unhampered by the dread presence of any outsider, lacking both in the support of tribal spirits as revealed in the customary phenomena of oneiromancy and epileptic ecphonema or through the interpretations of their witch-doctors, and in a leadership that inspired confidence.

Neither the agents nor the committee ever reported the obvious and elementary truth that the Bantu tribes would never be induced to rise at the call of doctrinaire preachifyings, and that though fascinated by engaging pledges dangled before their yearning gaze, before matters could be brought to a head and a general rebellion provoked, the African ideal had to be consolidated and local chiefs supplied to head it. On the other hand there is just as little doubt that, for the American negroes possessed and obsessed by this new phase in their evolution, the radiant vision of Ethiopia holding out her hands to God collapsed before that of Marcus Garvey's purple mantle, and their original frenzy for the apotheosis of a universal African Mother was transferred to the glorious one of an African republic or Kingdom under the rule of Marcus, overflowing with positions offering every chance for moral satisfaction coupled with earthly emblements which he could not fail to parcel out among his faithful supporters, which consciously or unconsciously they individually saw themselves snugly appropriating according to a personal appreciation of their merits, and to the greatest advantage of their profits.

The consequences of such a change of outlook in the direction of black nationalism led to a

ETHIOPIA A PAWN IN THE GAME

sharp repercussion in Africa, soon causing a blankness and a void in the hearts of the natives. Out of fear of competition from them, the Communists discountenanced local ringleaders of discontent and revolt, and Bishop Turner's exhortation to awake and arise was gradually construed into awake and look for orders to arise at the foreigner's bidding. Bishop Turner had ordained his apostles from members of their own tribes and Africans of Africa, with the implicit understanding that they were to work out the salvation of their own people. Instead the Socialists and Communists required them to credit the worth of rank outsiders and mercenary leaders, Africans of America or whites, on the bare assurance of unknown direction from abroad.

It did not take the expert long to recognize the symptomatic metamorphism of the natives' attitude, or the necessity of their spiritual revisualization before attempting to stir up a rebellion on a scale that might reasonably be expected to alter the distribution of African colonies, and give the Fatherland a chance to re-possess her old colonies, or annex new ones. The psychological errors committed by the agents of Bolshevism and their injudicious handling of nationalism had gone far to disintegrate a situation that up to a few years previously had appeared to be already welding together all elements, even the most antagonistic, into a solid anti-white front, and

THE SEETHING AFRICAN POT

these had to be rectified before the solution of Germany's problem could be attempted. And as it became abundantly evident that the deprivation of a purely African ideal had bitten deeply into the souls of the natives, an African pivot was deemed essential to the success of the enterprise. Strangely, unexpectedly perhaps, the most meticulous search could not discover one answering better to the purpose than the old Ethiopian ideal that for over thirty years had unfailingly set the strings of all African hearts vibrating.

Germans are methodical, profound, persevering and thorough. They vastly prefer to create a mechanism out of their own materials and fashion it to their liking; but they are also wonderfully cunning at turning to account the materials they have to hand, and have a marvellous gift for moulding them to their intentions. Once it was definitely established that Ethiopia was the one argument likely to prevail over the primitive tribes of Africa, that she was the one star they noticed in their firmament, they set about to revive the Ethiopian standard as the only one offering them likelihood of success.

Ethiopia was hauled out, so to speak, and laid on the dissecting table of cold rationalism and examined under political lenses for what she stood for in Africa, for what she was worth, for what she could do, and for what she would cost.

Ethiopia or Abyssinia, as she is called to-day,

though also styled Meroe or Nubia at various times throughout the centuries, rejoices in an origin dating back to time immemorial, and lost in the maze of uninscribed legends. In the opinion of some students of history her population is Hamitic and descended from some other part of Africa; others accept the Abyssinian tradition of a Semitic tribe that crossed from the Arabian peninsula about 5,000 years ago. However, the statements are so unsubstantiated that they cannot be counted as having any historical basis, which is a great comfort and offers wide scope to anybody wishing to ascribe to the Ethiopians some other adventure, one or more thousand years earlier. Ethiopia's grandeur in Egypt was already a thing of the past when it was recorded in the Old Testament, and as no other details are offered, there does not seem to be the slenderest probability of the debated question of its antecedents ever being cleared up by documentary proof.

Circa 992 B.C. the Queen of Sheba paid her visit to Solomon at Jerusalem, and though the Bible does not mention it, the Ethiopians claim her as Makeda, the reigning queen of Abyssinia at that time. The Chronicles say:

"And when she was come to Solomon she communed with him of all that was in her heart. . . . And when the Queen of Sheba had seen the wisdom of Solomon, and the house that he had built and the meat on his table," etc., "there was no more spirit in her."

It is a very delicate euphemism to describe how the haughty and barbaric queen, who had probably started out in the illusion of matching her riches and her wit against those of a sovereign whose reputation annoyed her, and of bringing it down a peg by "hard questions," had instead been overawed by the wealth and wisdom of the Israelite king, and very humanly succumbed to his manly charms.

All her "very great company" must have been equally overwhelmed, if after nearly 3,000 years Ethiopians are still proud of the son they are sure was born of the union of Makeda and Solomon. He was called Menelik and educated at the court of Solomon, his father, until he was eighteen years of age, when he was either recalled by his mother, or turned out by his father. Although it all happened so long ago, Abyssinians know all the details of his journey—how Menelik with the band of Abyssinians that formed his court succeeded in appropriating the Ark with the Tables of the Law and all its treasure and in escaping before the theft was discovered; but, impeded by the weight of it, were caught up by the cavalry that Solomon sent out in pursuit. Defending themselves as best they could, Menelik and his faithful party reached the shores of the Red Sea, where they discovered or were shown a secret tunnel leading to the African coast. This they bravely entered, thus putting an end to the chase, for divine intervention destroyed their traces, and their pursuers, not finding them or seeing any boat on the sea, concluded they had been drowned in an attempt to swim across. After this, for some unexplained motive, divine providence seems to have washed its hands of Menelik, and though allowing him to emerge safely from the secret tunnel, caused it to cave in, burying the Ark and all its contents before they had been drawn out. There is a general belief among Abyssinian Christians that if the site could be ascertained, properly conducted excavations would discover the Ark intact, and that the Ark the Israelites continued to worship was a substitute cleverly provided by Menelik, that passed unnoticed by the Israelite population whose deception was a dead secret that the priests dared not divulge.

In contradiction with this history is the fact that in Askum, the holy city of Ethiopia, an ark is preserved and worshipped as the True Ark, and the original one brought to Ethiopia by Menelik I. Little incongruities of this sort form no determent in any miracle-loving religion, and no satisfactory explanation can be hoped for. So one can only guess that the priests of Ethiopia may have found it expedient at some time to have an actual ark, and decided to follow the alleged example of the Israelites by having a fake made.

Christianity reached Ethiopia in A.D. 330, and

still exists in the Coptic form among those of the population known as Abyssinians proper.

According to Abyssinian tradition the descent from the union of Solomon and Makeda has been maintained in spite of frequent eclipses in its glory, which all proved transitory, for the reigning house has always been able to reassert itself. In A.D. 950 the Falasha tribe of Jews, claiming descent from Jacob, rebelled against the line of Solomon, murdered, as they thought, the whole royal family, and gained possession of the throne and the country, except the province of Shoa, whither one baby boy who had escaped the general massacre was conveyed secretly by a faithful retinue—a province over which he reigned after reaching the age of discretion, and where his descendants continued to reign after him.

Barely forty years afterwards the Falasha line of kings lost the throne to Zagues, another powerful Abyssinian, who also subjugated the whole country with the exception of the faithful province of Shoa where the Solomonian line continued to reign unopposed, without producing a member of any notable mettle until 1260 when the ruling king succeeded in recapturing all the territory his ancestors had lost.

Ethiopia, which up to A.D. 570 had ruled the Arabian province of Yemen, was in her turn attacked by Mohammedan hosts just after attaining her national unity again, and for about three

ETHIOPIA A PAWN IN THE GAME

centuries nobly withstood invasion repeatedly attempted. In the sixteenth century her strength failed her and the victorious Moslem fanatics overran the country, pillaging, murdering and torturing those who resisted conversion at the point of the scimitar. Numbers preferred death, or delayed in making up their minds too long for the short-tempered and fiery Moslems, who remorselessly cut them down, but thousands resigned themselves to forcible conversion, which after all had its compensations. Christianity was only saved from complete destruction in Ethiopia by the timely intervention of Cristoforo da Gama, a brother of the more famous Vasco, who with an inadequate following of less than five hundred men obliged wild hordes fantastically outnumbering his little band to retire. And this points the moral of the superiority of arms, training and discipline that the Abyssinians seem to have forgotten at the very moment they ought to have recalled and pondered it very soberly. The able use the Portuguese made of their thundering blunderbusses and their sapient manœuvring, wrought such havoc among the dense files of their opponents that the fanatical zeal oozed slowly out of the Mohammedan invaders, who retreated with more haste than dignity before the sonorous and deathly tactics that mowed them down. The house of Solomon ruled over a united Kingdom until 1813, after which for nearly

THE SEETHING AFRICAN POT

a century Ethiopia was split into six independent kingdoms, each under its own Ras, Shoa always continuing faithful to her historical dynasty until Menelik II, the Conquering Lion of Judah, reinstated his sway over the remaining Rasses, as Emperor, with the title of Negus Negasti, or King of Kings.

This development is not an unmixed blessing, nor is the imperial throne a comfortable or an easy seat, for the great Rasses are autocratic Kings ruling their subjects with mailed fist, and their allegiance to the Emperor is not to be trusted.

Abyssinia has no roads except about thirty miles from the capital, Addis Ababa, and her transport is all effected by caravans over ancient routes branching out in all directions. There is one railway 486 miles long from Jibuti, French Somaliland, to Addis Ababa; it is a one-metre gauge, and trains take three days to cover the distance, as they only run by day, though recently a weekly express doing the journey in thirty-six hours has been instituted. In the dry seasons the service is pretty regular. There is no census of the population in Abyssinia, and estimates vary according to personal conclusions rather than depend on any reliable information. In consequence it is reported to be anything from eight to eleven millions, but may be either more or less. It is very mixed, and includes many different peoples. The Abyssinians are the dominant race and the aristocracy, and look down on all the others, except the Falasha, as Shankalia or negroes. Religions also vary from the Coptic church of Abyssinia to Mohammedanism and pure unadulterated paganism. But one and all the tribes are wild and turbulent, living as much by robbery and raiding as by slave dealing, slave dealers just as soon seizing members of their own tribe when the chance offers, as of any other antagonistic one. It is a country where might is right and the law of claw and talon is as powerful as in any jungle.

Ethiopia's prestige in Africa consequent upon her triumphant success in repelling invasion, and in having remained unconquered throughout the centuries, is practically unfathomable. To the Africans in general, not only to those who invoked her as a liberator, she stands as a granite monument, a living exponent and testimony of the innate puissance of the black race, the shrine enclosing the last sacred spark of African political freedom, the impregnable rock of black resistance against white invasion, a living symbol, an incarnation of African independence.

The question of Ethiopia's assurance, how far confidence might safely be reposed in her, was a far more tricky question to answer. For the authority of the Negus, though ostensibly averred to be absolute, is in effect less substantial than is generally supposed, and depends entirely on the fealty of his under kings, the Rasses, for its support.

So that in reality what is often called the feudal system of Abyssinia corresponds exactly to the organization prevailing in the rest of primitive Africa, and the position of the Negus Negasti is precisely the same as that of a paramount chief of more southern peoples. That is to say, the Rasses must contribute to the upkeep of a general government, and recognize the authority of the Emperor in matters of the State as a whole and in its dealings with foreign nations; but in their own domains they, not the Negus, are the outstanding authorities. They exact taxes from their subjects, they are the direct overlords of the under, or smaller chiefs and the undisputed commanders of their armies.

To the populations in some of the outlying districts, over a month's journey from the capital and absolutely cut off from the rest of the world during the heavy rains, the actual Ras is the man to be feared and to be obeyed much more than a distant and shadowy Negus, so that though the Emperor is supposed to have control over the kings he has none directly over the subjects of those kings, who are in their turn the several props of his throne. As a defection of some big Ras would be a very serious matter and one not easily repaired, the Negus has to exercise much tact and diplomacy to keep his brittle mosaic in a state of cohesion, and his country in a semblance of order.

ETHIOPIA A PAWN IN THE GAME

When the proposal was broached to her, Ethiopia modestly hesitated to assume a responsibility of such magnitude as that of letting hell loose over Central Africa. She admitted having for years watched with the deepest interest the nascent nationalism of the primitive tribes and sympathizing with them in their troubles, sharing with them their hatred for the detestable white man, her heart beating patriotically in unison with those of all Africans yearning for freedom. She could not have been deaf to the cries for help that came to her from afar, but she had never seen her way to make a move in their favour. Besides, it was ridiculous of them to call her their mother; of course they were not her children. No Abyssinian mother, the descendant of the son of Solomon and Queen Makeda, could have nigger children. They were Shankalia, negroes, tribes she kept as slaves to work for her, to breed for her, to be lashed till the flesh fell off from their bones, to be chained in gangs and sold in the markets for her profit. This, naturally, would not have proved an obstacle, as she could not have any objection to enlarging her sphere of influence or her markets, but really she did not see how she could possibly accept the undertaking nor what benefit it would bring her. Oh yes, American negroes had visited her regularly and tried to enlist her support in their agitation. The besotted fools, not to know better than to expect a high-caste independent dame like herself, received on a par with all the civilized countries in the League of Nations, to demean herself by mixing with stinking Shankalia, clanking their chains and squabbling over the means of shaking themselves free from their serfdom. Naturally she had not neglected to maintain a sufficient number of students and observers in the principal countries of Europe, in America and Asia, to ensure being posted in all the latest developments, but Abyssinians never mixed with their inferiors, if you please.

On the other hand there might be a good deal of fun in heading a general African revolt, and her dear children were spoiling for a fight. They are such darlings when you understand them, but their overflowing spirits sometimes tempted them into high jinks that led them into trouble, and with three thousand miles of border in common with white administrations her hands were quite full enough. Besides, though *au fond* she quite approved their worrying and harassing their neighbours, a form of entertainment they were very partial to and found extremely profitable, they were perhaps hardly to be depended on for any regular enterprise.

The Russo-German secretariat ably parried these objections; Russia would furnish the means and Germany the brains of the enterprise. All Ethiopia need do was to be complacent and lend her name, and her new friends would see her safely through. They perfectly understood that she did not wish to be burdened with such a huge increase in her household and would be hard put to it to administer territories so far from her residence. However, if she consented to carry out their instructions, and accepted the part of figurehead of black nationalism and transmitted the signal for the rebellion when they sent it to her, they guaranteed the restitution of all her previous territories down to the Red Sea and Indian Ocean that she had lost at various times and to different States. As to the disintegrated tribes, if she would only hold them provisionally, Germany engaged later to take them off her hands and attend to them herself.

It was a daring scheme that required some time before it could be arranged and all the plans settled satisfactorily, yet everything seemed to concur in favour of the agreement. The great, the principal asset had been the fatuous admission of Ethiopia to the League of Nations, a step that opened to her previously undreamt-of vistas. She had already installed a Swedish Prime Minister and a Belgian mission to train her wild sons to a semblance of military discipline and the use of minor arms, which together with an appropriate supply of ammunition unobtrusively made its way in a small but steady stream to the country; and as the projected rebellion required some preparation and could not break out until convenient for Germany, it was hoped that Ethiopia would meanwhile have time to set up a regular army. Anyway, it was a start in the right direction, and with proper care the enterprise might be expected to develop finely.

Having efficiently persuaded Ethiopia to consent to play the part of the Great African Mother assigned to her, the secretariat focussed their attention on the other natives of Africa, to revive in them the dormant hopes of rebellion and freedom. Word was sent them that the great day they had so long expected was drawing near, when their long-deferred ambitions would materialize in a general rising under African leadership, during which they would freely indulge in the joy of massacring the whites and seizing those of their belongings they coveted. A steady seepage of arms and ammunition by the overland routes and through the ports of West Africa served by German shipping rallied their failing hearts and fed their enthusiasm, cases apparently of Italian spaghetti and macaroni proving invaluable for packing rifle barrels, while innocent-looking cases of Swiss condensed milk were a godsend for smuggling in small arms and ammunition under the unsuspecting noses of customs officials.

* * * * *

At this juncture there is a link missing in the chain of African events; it may be discovered

ETHIOPIA A PAWN IN THE GAME

later on, but at the present moment one must perforce be content to leap the small gap, of presumably a year or thereabouts, after which progress again becomes regular. The gap concerns the introduction of Japan on to the Ethiopian stage, for it is not clearly proved how, or when, she entered it. One thing is certain, she was firmly planted there in 1933. However, the actual gap may be usefully filled up by a cursory glance at Japan's position at home and in Africa. Her problems at home are so magisterially exposed in *Empire in the East*, edited by Joseph Barnes, that a brief quotation from that invaluable book [1] will give a clear understanding of them.

Empire in the East, p. 46.

"With the throwing off of the constrictions that had hampered the country during the feudal period, one of the most striking results has been the rapid increase of the population. Since 1873 it has doubled, and in 1932 the increase was a little over one million. In view of the limited area of the country, Japan is faced with a serious population problem. In a territory smaller than the state of California, there is a population of almost sixty-seven million, or a density of 450 per square mile. Five-sixths of the country, however, because of its rugged mountainous topography, is not arable, and the population density in relation to the area that can be utilized for agriculture is some 27,000

[1] By kind permission of the publishers, Kegan Paul & Co.

per square mile. No other important country is quite so crowded.

(p. 53) "The climate of Japan is well suited to the cultivation of the cotton plant, and at the time of the opening of the country it was a crop of such importance that many of the early foreign visitors predicted that Japan would shortly become one of the leading sources of raw cotton for the textile mills of the world. But little cotton is grown at present. The demand upon the arable land for food crops has been too great, and practically all the raw cotton now consumed in Japanese cotton industry is obtained in U.S.A., India, China and Egypt.

(p. 63) "The leading manufacturing industry at the present time is the textile industry. It includes the reeling of raw silk, cotton spinning, cotton weaving, and the weaving of silk and mixed cloth, the spinning and weaving of wool, hemp, flax and other fibres, and the finishing of cloth. This group of industries employs about half of all the factory workers, and contributes some 45% of the total value of all manufactured goods and two-thirds of the value of Japanese exports.

(p. 65) "Because of the scarcity of resources within the Empire Japanese manufacturing from the beginning of the modern period has been dependent to a very large extent upon imports for its raw materials. The rapid growth of industry is reflected in the increase in the value of imports from an average of 31,000,000 yen per year in the period just prior to 1880, to 1·8 billion yen for the five years ending with 1932. The most significant item in the import trade at present is raw cotton. From a minor position in the earlier years it has advanced both absolutely and relatively and now represents from 25 to 30% of the total import trade. . . .

(p. 67) "In the earlier years, cotton textiles, silk tissues and clothing were the principal items of import. In the exports, they constituted less than 0·5% of the total. Today they have become insignificant in the import trade, and the group of textile products, including raw silk, cotton yarn and cloth, silk tissues and clothing, account for from 65 to 75% of the exports. As Japanese trade has developed, the exports have formed two major streams. Raw silk, a luxury product, has gone to the U.S.A., and the textile staples, cotton especially, have gone to the countries of Asia.

"At present these two markets take about 80% of the export trade. . . . It is in the textile industries that the most promising opportunities for industrial expansion are presented, and it is upon Japan's ability to market abroad its textile products that its future as an industrial nation depends. . . .

(p. 69) "One of Japan's greatest advantages for industrialization long viewed with envy by Western manufacturers is a dense population with a low standard of living that provides factory labour at low wages. It is true that much of this labour is unskilled and inefficient, and labour costs have been high despite low wages. With experience, efficiency has improved, and the introduction of the newer and automatic machinery has made skill a less significant consideration. At the same time there has been no compensating rise in wages, and labour costs are becoming lower and lower. It is an advantage that Japan should continue to enjoy, certainly in comparison with occidental nations, since it is not likely that there will be any immediate advance in wages. In the last few years they have declined. There is even the possibility that they may be pushed still lower in the next decade or so, when there will be from the present annual increase in population a net addition every year of some 450,000 or 500,000 to the number of individuals seeking employment."

Japan slipped into Africa with all tactical unobtrusiveness, mostly through white agents, and she kept so well hidden in the background that her presence was not realized for a long time by the whites in Africa, and is not credited at all by the thingamabob tin gods of Europe, who still fondly believe that their pleasure and their will shall rule the destinies of the whole terrestrial globe. It is a dangerous fallacy persevered in by the crowds and not to be overcome as long as the sale of serious books lags badly behind that of detective stories, and the cinema is their ultimate goal of life. It is a notable peculiarity of Europeans really to believe that what is of supreme importance to them must interest the rest of humanity to the same extent, and inversely, that what does not strike them as noteworthy cannot be worthy of notice. A curious instance of this is given in the conviction with which they speak and write about the "world war," which sounds as if the conflict that raged in Europe had really

ETHIOPIA A PAWN IN THE GAME

spread to the whole world, and in their deplorable ignorance of the surprise that this way of describing what after all was a very circumscribed affair causes in the other continents. To the Far Easterns and to the Africans Europe is so distant, and the war so remote, that those not personally concerned in it hardly realized that it was on at all, and even those natives who were dragged into it in the various African colonies understood it as a local squabble between whites. To the Japanese as a nation there is something pitifully comic in the size of the swelled heads of Europe, whose inhabitants they call merely "whites," without the least concern as to their particular place of origin. For them the war in China is of much more vital interest than any disruption in Europe, and they naturally sniff more and more at European presumption as time passes and they advance in importance as a factor in the trade of the world.

In Africa, barring the natives who have visited other continents, a very few of the better-educated ones, or the highest and most progressive chiefs, the whites are just "Europeans," even those of African nationality, like the whites of South Africa, or the Americans. Pretty well as Europeans speak of the Africans as if they were one people, so do the Africans, when speaking of the whites, soar above such petty details of distinction as political nationality.

THE SEETHING AFRICAN POT

According to many considered opinions Japan decided on an African economic invasion about 1925–26, for by 1927 she had become active there. She began by concluding what trade agreements she could, by dumping her goods wherever it was permitted her, and organizing by every ruse their infiltration into countries where they were excluded. Politically, she craftily insinuated into a certain element in the Union of South Africa the patriotic ambition for their country to denounce membership of the British Commonweath and declare itself an Independent Republic which, with an immense length of undefendable coastline, a small army of untrained territorial battalions, and no navy, would be open to invasion at a fortnight's notice. Yet so cleverly did Japan pull the strings that such a project incredibly found a small party in the country to uphold it and seriously recommend its adoption.

Whoever may care to investigate this point further could do no better than read, and ponder *The Yellow Man Looks On*, by Hedley A. Chilvers, a book published in 1933, when the great excitement over the attempted Japanese settlement in the Union of South Africa had only just abated. Hedley A. Chilvers is a very well-known writer in South Africa, whose several books on his country form extremely interesting reading. In the case of *The Yellow Man Looks On*, any doubt about the accuracy of his statements can be laid to rest as he

ETHIOPIA A PAWN IN THE GAME

has had the immense advantage of a foreword by Sir Abe Bailey, the South African gold magnate, a man whose opinion carries such immense weight also in England. Sir Abe Bailey opens his foreword with the solemn declaration that he wholly concurs with Mr. Chilvers.

In *The Yellow Man Looks On* Mr. Chilvers briefly sketches the troubled internal condition of the Union of South Africa, the bitter rivalry and deep hate dividing the two leading white races in the land, namely the Dutch, or Boers, and the English. He draws a very melancholy picture of the prolonged dissensions and profound antagonism between the two, and admonishes that settlement of their differences, national unity, and to remain within the British Commonwealth are three essential conditions for the Union's existence.

Further, very clearly and with unequivocal sincerity he tells the story of Japan's efforts to gain a footing in the Union, and tries to awaken his fellow citizens to their imminent danger from persevering on a course he does not hesitate to declare a direct incitement to the Yellow Man, whom he describes as eager and sinister, watching South Africa from his overcrowded islands with yearning, and only waiting for a favourable opportunity to step in.

According to Mr. Chilvers the first warning of Japanese interest in the Union was apparently given by a correspondent of the *Star* of Johannesburg, who returned in 1927 from a visit to Japan with the news that the Japanese Bureau of Population and Food Investigation were advising an attempt to induce the Government of the Union to allow an outlet of the Japanese surplus population within the territory of the Union. But nothing more seems to have been said on the subject until July 7, 1931, when the *Rand Daily Mail*, which Mr. Chilvers describes as the leading morning organ of the gold-fields, startled its readers with the unexpected information that Japanese agents from Capetown were trying to acquire by private contract a large property known as the Bar R Ranch in the Usutu valley, with the view of forming a Japanese settlement. The names of these agents were not published, and they were described as doing everything in their power towards maintaining the transactions secret, declining to give interviews or any information.

The whole population of the Union went into an uproar, for the Bar R Ranch is 267 square miles, has 120,000 acres under cotton, can further yield fair crops of tobacco, maize and sugar, and, worst of all, it was estimated that it could support something like the amazing figure of 80,000 Japanese. The ranch is only 70 miles from Mbabane, the capital of Swaziland, and in size is equal to the territories of the two republics of San Marino and Andorra combined, or four times the combined territories of the two principalities of Monaco and Lichtenstein. Mr. Chilvers tells how an old law dating as far back as 1885 forbidding the sale of land to Asiatics was then unearthed, and as it had been extended to Swaziland in 1907, the transactions for the sale of the Bar R Ranch came to an abrupt end.

Japan, however, did not relinquish completely her designs on the Union, and she succeeded in conducting negotiations with the Government of the Union for a Commercial Treaty, or Agreement, with such secrecy that all leakage was avoided, and the first intimation the public had of the affair was the news that the Agreement was signed.

This time, too, Mr. Chilvers tells us, the public was very much upset and the outcry was very great although it was too late to prevent its accomplishment. Mr. Chilvers kindly gives a list of 17 Chambers of Commerce belonging to all four provinces of the Union that formally protested against the Treaty. He also quotes the *Cape Times* as follows: "Even if S. Africa were wholly white there would still be adequate reasons for maintaining the policy of Asiatic exclusion which the Union has deliberately followed since its foundation." According to Mr. Chilvers the greatest fears were then entertained that Japan might start a chain of stores throughout the land, but they had not materialized yet at the time of his writing.

THE SEETHING AFRICAN POT

Mr. Chilvers states roundly his conviction that Japan is hankering for an opportunity to insinuate part of her surplus population in a country whose own rate of population per mile is one of the lowest, especially as its climate is considered to be favourable to the Japanese constitution. As Mr. Chilvers justly remarks, Japan is practically at her wits ends to find a solution for her population problem, and it is hardly probable that it lies in the already overcrowded Chinese provinces she has recently annexed. Mr. Chilvers considers it only natural that, given her population problem, Japan should cast covetous glances on sparsely populated areas, but he also examines at some length the temptation that the rich gold fields, coal mines, tin mines, and other mineral wealth of the Union must be to Japan, and he declares them treasures well worth fighting for, betraying a certain concern for the possibility, if not the probability, that at some not specified date Japan may consider it worth her while to do so. Therefore he urges his fellow countrymen to cease from internal strifes and feuds so weakening to the country, and upholds the vital necessity for the Union of South Africa to remain within the Commonwealth and enjoy the protection of the British fleet.

Given the personality of the author himself, *The Yellow Man Looks On* is a very precious book, for Mr. Chilvers is too careful, and too well

ETHIOPIA A PAWN IN THE GAME

known a writer to indulge in literary vapourings. He could only utter such grave warnings after due reflection. But when added to that, he obtains a foreword to his book from Sir Abe Bailey, one of South Africa's greatest and most prominent men, who begins his foreword ominously: "I concur with the author's views," *The Yellow Man Looks On* sounds a very tocsin for the Yellow peril in Africa. This also is a phrase of Sir Abe Bailey's, for he considers the yellow peril one of the main reasons for the Union's necessity to remain within the British Commonwealth. For Japan, according to Sir Abe Bailey, represents an "aggressive military menace to the peace of the world." Sir Abe Bailey further expresses the opinion that Africa may well be the battlefield where the East and the West may clash some day in a decisive conflict, and he adds his admonishments to those of Mr. Chilvers entreating his readers to forbear from steps that might allow Japan a chance one day to lay waste the flourishing towns of South Africa. Indeed, in Sir Abe Bailey's own words, "reduce our towns to smouldering ruins."

However, the fairest field for Japanese enterprise in Africa was offered by Ethiopia, and once the two countries made contact they fell into each other's arms locked in a passionate embrace, united by the bond of common hatred for the white man. From the moment of setting foot in the Black Continent, Japan had taken the keenest

THE SEETHING AFRICAN POT

interest in all things African, tentatively prodding at all points in the effort to introduce the thin end of her wedge, like Germany trusting to luck for an opportunity to push it in some time. Ethiopia with her ambitions aroused provided the occasion, and by pampering these, Japan succeeded in bringing off a veritable masterstroke, completely to her own advantage, although she managed cleverly to wrap it up to appear as a favour to Ethiopia.

Relations between the two countries had been cordial for some years before official visits were exchanged between Tokyo and Addis Ababa, which resulted immediately in a commercial treaty, with a political one following closely on its heels. The millions of Ethiopians clad or rather enveloped in flowing robes, the populace in cotton, the rich or pretentious in silk, were glad of the opportunity of acquiring their material at much cheaper rates than they had as yet enjoyed; and for Japan struggling to find new markets which would save her from being smothered by her own super-production, that of Ethiopia relieved her of the burden crushing her chest.

In 1933, at the same time that her underhand influence was causing great uneasiness to the observers and thinkers in the Union of South Africa, Japan concluded a political treaty with Ethiopia, the clauses of which, with one exception, have been kept as secret as possible, though

ETHIOPIA A PAWN IN THE GAME

a certain leakage has been inevitable. Rumour is notoriously a lying jade, but when facts confirm her information it is wise to go warily before condemning her gossip.

The one clause referred to was the grant of 400,000 hectares of Ethiopian soil to Japan for the cultivation of cotton, and a monopoly of the opium poppy, labour to be supplied by Japan. For Japan's desperate need of a vent for her surplus population dovetails exactly with Ethiopia's peculiar plight, for her redoubtable, elegant and lithe warrior sons, in the overweening vanity of their aristocracy and prowess, refuse to stoop to manual labour. Hence their necessity for slaves to carry on the work of the country, and the reason why the abolition of slavery in Ethiopia demands either an evolution towards civilization that must inevitably be a slow one, or an outside, trenchant authority powerful enough to impose a complete moral and material upheaval on a fierce and haughty race.

In this way the acute Far-Eastern Empire secured at one stroke the stable footing in the African Continent she hankered for, and the outlet for her population, besides assuring the future independence of her supplies of raw materials for her cotton and opium trades from foreign markets.

Now is the moment to listen to the gossip of that busy jade, Rumour, for what she has to say, though not published in any official document, stands so well the test of events that it is well worth listening to.

The weakness of Ethiopia's preparations in case of war against any white army could not escape the notice of so astute a country as Japan, and she delicately drew Ethiopia's attention to the fact that she was not equipped to resist the impact of even the weakest of them. Ethiopia has only recently instituted a regular corps of a very few thousand strong at the direct disposal of the Negus, formed of men trained by the Belgian mission, provided with modern arms and broken in to a certain military discipline, such as may be considered rather a nucleus out of which an army may grow than as an army in itself. The remainder of her forces is constituted by the untutored hordes, followers of the under-kings, or provincial Rasses; warriors eager for any fray and of a stuff from which first-rate soldiers are made, but neither properly armed nor at all trained according to the rules of modern warfare, and not dependable for longer than the spirit moves them to continue fighting.

Throughout the whole of Central and Southern Africa native tactics have been the same for the past century. Guerilla warfare to harass and exhaust the advancing enemy while deploying and retreating in a manner to lead them into some ambush; or surprise massed attacks one hour before dawn, besides as much private sniping and mutilation of dead and wounded as each warrior finds an opportunity for. If the attack is successful the war is over, the enemy put to flight, and the conquering army either settles down on the land, or pillages and raids it to its heart's content before returning home with a light conscience to enjoy the proceeds of victory. In case of defeat the invaders generally give up and retreat; very rarely they have rallied for a second attempt. Indeed, as a rule they retreat as quickly as possible, thankful when pursuit does not follow on their disaster, though they must keep constantly on the alert for avenging parties once they are home.

With the keenest diplomatic regret Japan considered it her duty further to point out to Ethiopia the difficulty of keeping her army together in the event of a Ras becoming huffy and removing himself from the action, or of his concluding a separate peace much to his own advantage; as also the need to foresee the danger of the whole army becoming panic-stricken at its first experience of air-bombing, of tanks and the further appliances of civilized and progressive destruction, or of its dissolving in a night under the friendly protection of darkness. She, Ethiopia, ought not to forget that her sons spoke of war in terms of rifles, stones and spears, and that they could not be blamed if they were overcome by unreasoning terror at forms of attack hitherto unknown, that must appear to them to be due to some supernatural enemy that they were powerless to resist. Might she, Japan, suggest without offence that her dear friend Ethiopia should reconsider her plight were she to go to war with a white country; might they not discuss the position together, and perhaps find a solution? Paucity of exact details concerning the transactions that led to the completion of the Nippo-Ethiopian treaty can again safely be supplemented by hypothesis, for they are ultimately authenticated by the logical testimony of occurrences and phenomena prevailing throughout Africa by 1933.

Rumour whispered, "The agreements between Germany and Ethiopia on one hand, and between Japan and Ethiopia on the other, have been fused into a tripartite treaty including all three countries. Ethiopia and Japan will fight Germany's battles in Africa while she is engaged in Europe, and then they will all sit round in happy celebration of their victory over the common enemy."

As this may seem preposterous to people unacquainted with the developments in Africa after the advent of Nazi-ism as the ruling power in Germany, a summary of them is apposite. One of the first cares of Nazi-ism was to assume direct command over her citizens abroad and to incorporate them into the party willy-nilly—often distinctly nilly. At eighteen boys and girls are automatically absorbed into it and must start heil-hitlering with the rest. The ideals of German nationalism and the necessity of German vindication in Africa are decanted all over the place with a unanimity of phraseology distinctly smacking of circular instructions. German citizens in the Mandated Provinces fly the German flag professing to have no other in a way that suggests orders from headquarters. Revilement of the Jews and private persecution of them has been instituted and is in operation to the fullest extent possible, while the Greyshirt organization has introduced into the land the custom of public insult and assault of the Jews.

The whole scope of this complex and coordinate activity tends to create in Africa an atmosphere favourable to the restitution to Germany of the colonies she has been deprived of, or alternatively giving her others. Neither pains nor expense are spared in this intensive propaganda for whose realization a date was already fixed in 1934; such at least was the conviction repeatedly and openly affirmed by many Germans in Africa and their supporters.

They all of them announced that Germany would have her preparations for war ready in 1937 or 1938 at the latest, and that while she was engaging the European powers in another continental war they, in combination with a general rising of the natives in all regions, of which they are positively confident, would wipe off from the fair face of Africa the present blot on her landscape presented by the actual distribution of colonies.

Early in October all the principal papers published the following Reuter telegram:

"Moshi (Tanganyika), September 28.

" 'Peaceful penetration' back into what was previously a part of German East Africa is being continued steadily by German settlers in the northern province of Tanganyika.

"They are steadily buying up British owned farms, and are, incidentally, doing great harm to British trade interests in the territory. They buy goods in Germany, export them, and sell them here at cut-throat prices. Cement is a favoured article for this purpose. British cement costs, up country, 18*s.* 6*d.* per cask, whereas a good brand of German cement which was previously sold at about the same price can now be obtained for 15*s.*

"The result is disturbing. In certain districts where British farms were once in the majority, German owners are now predominant."

In 1934 about 150 farms passed into German hands, besides trading stations. This "peaceful penetration" is in prevision of the day when a census of the white population of Tanganyika will be taken for the use of the League.

As far as this it is easy to get them to talk of their beautiful programme, but at this point they shrivel up and change the subject. They refuse to discuss the situation from the point of view of the deluded blacks, or what may be the consequences the day they understand its purport. The rain, drought, locusts, poetry or any other subject will be introduced and firmly adhered to, or changed to some other equally innocent, but the conversation can never be switched back to German plans of vindication in Africa. On her side, after having accomplished the task she had set herself of persuading Ethiopia of the futility and danger to herself in engaging in her enterprise unless she made wider preparations, Japan proceeded to unfold her plans.

She herself was on the horns of a dilemma, for while her own overcrowded population required new camping grounds, there was another very grave problem with a difficult solution for the Japanese authorities to face. Statistics prove that Japanese migration in the European acceptance of the word, of people leaving their homes and being assimilated somewhere else, acquiring land or a business and rearing families as future citizens of their adopted country, is a failure. There is something in the physical, moral or psychological constitution of the Japanese that prevents them in the main from settling down permanently in any other country; migration for them is nothing more than a temporary absence from their own country, as some urge will suddenly force them to give up regular and comfortable circumstances to return home, although perfectly aware of the danger of having to face famine once they have consumed their savings. This fact has proved itself time and again with people voluntarily living in the most favourable surroundings, and it would therefore be still more marked when the current of migration was artificially propelled towards Africa, where the conditions were so opposite to their home environment that Nature herself spontaneously erected inviolate barriers to miscegenation and xenogamy between all Asiatics, whether Mongols or Indians, and Africans.

So clear a perception of the obstacles besetting her path and on the surface compromising the success of her settlement in Ethiopia might have caused uneasiness to Japan at some other moment, but owing to the peculiar situation it suggested the happiest and easiest solution of many perplexities and proved itself a heaven-sent help for her chances. Abandoning with characteristic promptitude her original scheme of attempting to compel her citizens to a permanent colonization in Ethiopia, Japan decided instead to send out those thousands of cotton and opium growers required for a short time of service, and to renew them by detachments in order gradually to substitute the whole lot through a continual rotation. These men, besides their ostensible business of cotton and opium growing, would be fully trained and equipped soldiers completely officered, constituting a small but very efficient and reliable modern army at the service of Ethiopia in the unhappy event of war against any of her white neighbours who might lose a long-tried temper. Japan also could engage to send war aircraft when hostilities broke out, if Ethiopia meanwhile provided herself with a few aeroplanes, so as to furnish the excuse for making those preparations that demand time, namely, preparing landing-places, laying in provisions of fuel, etc.

Of course Japan would consider herself entitled to an adequate recompense after rendering such signal services, and Ethiopia agreeing, a flourishing port in the Red Sea with sufficient hinterland to guarantee a safe naval base was stipulated as eventual payment. How far are these rumours apocryphal, or what epexegetical evidence do they bring that it is not simply malingering?

The official returns of the port of Jibuti show that Japan imported goods into Abyssina during the year 1934 to the tune of 8,650,000 fr., more than double those of France who is next on the list with only 3,260,000 fr., leaving Great Britain a poor third with 1,705,000 fr. These figures prove of themselves that Japan has won the race as far as Ethiopia's import market is concerned. The Manchester bulletin of master cotton spinners for 1935 states that Japan's cotton spinning companies showed average dividends of 12 per cent for the year 1934, not a bad figure compared with European returns. By this of course it is not meant that all Japan's cotton now goes to Ethiopia, but these figures do show how for the last year at least Japan has dominated Abyssinian markets.

The same unfortunately may be said for Abyssinia's exports, where Japan again is first on the list.

Whereas the other white countries in general dissociated themselves from African internal affairs, Germany, the only one to interest herself in them deeply for personal reasons, hailed with delight these developments so largely to her own advantage. Her friendship for Japan was renewed very soon after the great war, and has often been alluded to by the German press that only expresses official opinion, and has recently and repeatedly compared the situation of Germany and Japan as countries equally victimized by the hostility of the other Great Powers, denying them their rights and refusing to recognize their necessity for expansion.

All factors taken into due consideration, one can safely conclude that Japan, besides a colony in Africa, counts on getting a naval base in the Red Sea which will permit her to weigh more heavily in the scales of international, and especially of European affairs than she has been able to do hitherto, and of becoming a thorn festering in

ETHIOPIA A PAWN IN THE GAME

the flesh of European countries with interests in and beyond the Suez Canal. Germany hopes to regain some colonies in Africa through the medium of Ethiopia, planning to fire the fuse when she herself is ready to engage the European countries at home. But as she has candidly confessed that she will not be ready until 1937 or '38, and neither Japan nor Ethiopia is prepared to face the situation two or three years earlier than planned, having an issue forced on them at this moment is particularly disagreeable as it upsets their deeply-laid conspiracy. Ethiopia especially deserves consideration, for with her inexperience, ingenuousness and trust in her new friends she never suspects that the caressing hands, so gently stroking her now, are slowly creeping towards her windpipe, and that they may one day choke her without even giving her time to see whether the hands that perpetrate the deed are white and podgy or lean and yellow.

APPENDIX I

CHURCH ACTIVITIES IN NUMBERS

These missions are quoted because their reports happen to come to hand; others are just as bad, and may be counted on for doing their worst.

Jesuits in the Kwango for 1928, a district seven times the size of Belgium, with 1,000,000 inhabitants. The priests are 45.

	Catholics.	Catechumens.
1907	4·145	4·125
1914	9·184	3·891
1921	20·142	23·705
1926	50·015	62·804

This is an excerpt of the report published in 1928.

Missionaries in the Benguela hinterland are called by the natives Afulu, probably a corruption of the word fools which they have heard from unsympathetic whites along the coast.

APPENDIX II

THE WAHELE REBELLION

The Iringa district of Tanganyika is the home of a very warlike tribe of the Wahele, a raiding tribe which in 1891 defeated the Von Zelesky punitive expedition, thereby establishing for itself a name for invincibility and for its paramount chief a reputation for possessing supernatural powers. As a result Mkwawa, this Wahele chief, raided right and left, sometimes personally, quite often more comfortably by means of deputies nobody dared to resist. Even white caravans were obliged to submit to his extortions and pay tribute before venturing to pass near his domain, much less adventure into it.

Matters continued in this way till 1894 when Col. Von Schele was despatched on another punitive expedition formed of five companies of troops commanded by 16 white officers and 17 white N.Cs. After 6 days' march the column reached Mkwawa's capital, Kuirengu, a fortified town situated astride the river Ruaha, completely surrounded by a wall 12 feet high and 8 miles in circumference, with bastions 300 yards apart from each other.

Their artillery being insufficient to bombard the town, the assailers had to scale the walls. They met with the most determined resistance, and only after prolonged fighting, said to have cost the Germans about 60 men, the stronghold capitulated. Mkwawa made good his escape, but the victors took much booty, estimated at 2,000 head of cattle and 30,000 pounds of gunpowder.

The Wahele warriors rallied immediately to the extent of harassing the retreat of the Germans, but all Mkwawa's efforts in this line were ineffectual. However, he still refused to submit and kept up a desultory guerila warfare that became such a menace that the Germans had to take further measures for subduing the rebel paramount chief. Pursuing troops kept him in continual motion, while his country was divided up and given in charge of other chiefs as it fell into the hands of the authorities. A price of 1,000 rupees was placed on the head of Mkwawa, but by this time he had become a national hero and not one of his tribesmen were tempted by the reward. Daring, resourceful, beloved, he slipped in and out between the patrols sent out to effect his capture, who were often so close on his heels that they found fresh provisions laid out for him in the forests. A couple of times that they caught him up some of his followers would engage the troops in skirmish, giving up their lives to provide the means of his escape. This state of affairs lasted until July 1889 and only ended then because Mkwawa fell in the forest.

A detachment that happened to be near heard of his illness and plunged into the forest with all precaution, creeping along and climbing trees to discover their quarry. At last they heard two shots ring out quite near, and crawling along in the direction whence

APPENDIX II

they came, finally saw a smoking fireplace and two figures lying close to it. Those they shot at before rushing up, only to discover that the men had been dead about an hour. One of the bodies was recognized as that of Mkwawa. The most plausible explanation seems to be that the rebel chief had heard the detachment advancing, or had been warned of its approach, and Mkwawa not being in a condition to flee, had shot himself, probably first shooting his last remaining friend who presumably had elected to follow his cherished leader up to the end.

The corpse of Mkwawa was recognized by several people before it was buried, the natives as they arrived standing in grief-struck silence to contemplate it for several minutes, as if paying it homage. Before burying it, the Non. C. in command cut off the head to take back in proof of his exploit, and afterwards it is supposed to have been sent to Berlin for exhibition in a museum. Some natives credit this version, whereas others believe that the true skull was stolen as an object of worship for his bereaved followers, and another skull substituted in its place, as a fake.

With Mkwawa's death the country settled down peacefully, nor has it given any more trouble, excepting over the matter of the skull. In 1919 the Wahele were still attaching so much importance to it, that a clause was inserted in the Treaty of Versailles binding the Germans to give it back. The skull apparently cannot be traced so the clause has not been fulfilled, and the Wahele are still agitating for it.

APPENDIX III

NATIVE SEPARATIST CHURCHES, 1933, REGISTERED BY THE GOVERNMENT OF THE UNION OF SOUTH AFRICA [1]

African Native Catholic Church
African Faith Mission
African Catholic Bantu Church
African Methodist Episcopal Church
African Methodist Church of South Africa
African Baptist Sinoia Church
African Zulu Methodist Church
African Zion Baptist Church
African Lutheran Church
African Mission House Church
African Holy Catholic Church
African Holy Baptist Church of South Africa
African Seventh Day Adventists
African Christian Christ Church
African Seventh Church of God
African Pentecostal Baptist Church

[1] I have to acknowledge the courtesy of the Editor, J. Merle Davis, Esq., and of Messrs Macmillan, the publishers, to quote this valuable material from *Modern Industry and the African*.

APPENDIX III

African Pentecostal Faith Mission
African Catholic Church of South Africa
African Christian Catholic Baptist Church
African Reform Church
African Christian Apostolic Church (2 churches)
African Mission Society
African Free Catholic Church
African Free Bapedi Church
African National Baptist Church Association
African Orthodox Apostolic Church
African Presbyterian Bafolisi Church
African Evangelistic Band
African Native Mission Church
African Native Free Church
African Christian Church
African Empumulanga Mission
African Congregational Church
African Province Church
African Independent Baptist Church
African Independent Apostle Church
African United Church
African United Ethiopian Church
African Bethel Mission
African Congress Catholic Church
African United Brethren Church of St. Moravian
Africa Church
African United Zulu Congregational Church
African Mission Catholic Church
African Christian Missionary Church
African National (Bethel) Baptist Church
African Baptist Mission Church
African United Gaza Church
African Pentecostal Mission

THE SEETHING AFRICAN POT

African Catholic Episcopal Church
African Sabbath Mission Church
African Seventh Day Zulu Chaka Church of Christ
African Mission Church
African Native Mission Church
African Native Methodist Church
African Bakgatla National Church
African Native Apostle Church
African Free Congregational Church
African Independent Mission Church
African Orthodox Church
African Congregational Methodist Church
African Catholic Church of Gaza
African Catholic Mission
African Holy Messenger Church in Zion
African Cathedral Episcopal Church
African Baptist Church in Zion
African Baptist Sinoia Apostolic Church Beira
African Pentecostal Church
African Ethiopian Church
African Christian Baptist Church of South Africa
African Bavenda Church
Afrikaanse Natieve Evangelie Kerk
Allmount Mount of Olives Baptist Church
American Ethiopian Church
American Christian Church
Ama Yoyopiya
Amakushe
Assemblies of God Church
Afro–Athlican Constructive Gaathly
Apostle Church of the Full Bible of South Africa
Apostle Church in Zion
Apostles and Christian Brethren Church

APPENDIX III

Abyssinian Baptist Church
Algemene Volks Kerk
Apostolic Church Messenger in Zion
Apostolic Faith Church
Apostolic Faith Assembly
Apostolic Heaven Church in Zion
Apostolic South African Zulu Church
Apostolic Baptist Church in Zion
Apostolic Church of Zion in South Africa
Apostolic Brethren Church
Apostolic Faith Assembly
Apostolic Holy Messenger Church in Zion
Apostolic Holy Zion Mission in South Africa
Apostolic Assembly Faith Church of South Africa
Apostolic Church in Zion of the New Jerusalem Mission in Basutoland
Apostolic Messenger Light World Church in Zion
Apostolic Jerusalem Church in Sabbath
Apostolic Church in Zion Amen
Apostolic United African Church of South Africa
Bethel Church
Brethren Mission Church
Bechuan Methodist Church
Bechuana Methodist in Zion
Bethel Apostolic Baptist Church
Bethesda Zion Apostolic Church of Africa
Basuto Redemption Episcopal
Berean Bible Readers' Society
Bantu Ngcqiki—Witsikana Church
Bantu Baptist Church
Bantu Presbyterian Church of South Africa
Baptist Church of the Seventh Day Adventists of Africa

Baptist of the Seventh Day Adventists
Bible Standard Church of America
Catholic African Union
Christian Apostolic Heaven Church in Zion
Christian Catholic Apostolic Church in Zion
Christian Bavenda Church of South Africa
Christian Brethren
Christian Apostolic Church in Zion
Christian Bethlehem Church
Christian Church Mission of South Africa
Christian Apostolic Zulu Churches of Zion
Chaka Zulu Church
Church of God and Saints of Christ
Church of Christ
Church of the Holy Kingdom of Christ the Saviour
Church of Africa Mission House (Homes)
Church of Christ from the Union of the Bantu
Church of Christ in South Africa
Church of Israel
Church of God
Church of the Nazarenes
Church of the Prophets
Church of the Christian Evangelists
Mission Church of Israel
Church of the Holy Ghost
Congregational Union African Church
Congregational Church of Christ
Congregational Gaza Church
Die Namakwa Independente Kerk van Zuid Afrika
Ethiopia Church Lamentation of South Africa
Ethiopian Catholic Church of Zion in South Africa
Ethiopian Church
Ethiopian Catholic Church of South Africa

APPENDIX III

Ethiopian Baptist Church of South Africa
Ethiopian Mission of South Africa
Ethiopian Church of Basutoland
Ethiopian Methodist Church of South Africa
Ethiopian Church of God the Society of Paradise
Ethiopian Orthodox Catholic Church
Ethiopian Messenger Catholic Church in South Africa
Epifania African Church
East African Gaza Church
Episcopal Egreja Luzo Africana Church
Ethiopia Church of Abyssinia
East Heathlon Church
Evangelist Catholic Church
East Star Baptist Church of Portuguese East Africa
Empumalanga Gospel Church
Free Methodist Episcopal Church
Full Gospel Church
Filadelfia Church of Africa
First Catholic Apostolic Church Jerusalem in Zion of South Africa
First Church of God Asia in Efese Church in South Africa
First Native Church of Christ
Gospel Messenger Church
Griqua Independent Church
Gazaland Zimbabwe Ethiopian Church
General Convention Church of New Jerusalem
Heaven Apostolic Jerusalem Church in Zion
Holy Catholic Episcopal Church
Heaven Twelfth Apostle Church
Holy National Church of South Africa
Home Natives Co-operative Society
Hephzibah Faith Mission Association

THE SEETHING AFRICAN POT

Holy Missionary Evangelistic Church
Holy Apostolic Church
Holy Catholic Apostolic Church in Zion
Holy Sabbath Church
International Missionary Alliance
International Holiness Church
International Baptist Church of God
International Foursquare Gospel
Independent Church of South Africa
Independent Native Presbyterian Church
Independent and United National Church
Independent Methodist Church of Africa
Intercommunion Church of South Africa
Independent Ethiopian Congress Mission
Independent Presbyterian Church
Independent or Congregational Church
Jerusalem Christian Church in Zion of South Africa
King of Salom Melchizedeck Church
Kush Nineveh Church
Kush Apostolic Church
Lutheran Bapedi Church
Lott Carey Baptist Mission of South Africa
Magana National Church Association.
Methodist Episcopal Church
Methodist African Church
Metropolitan Church Association
Mayen Church
Modern Mission
Mount Zion A. M. E. Church
New Apostle Church
Nazarenes (or Shembites)
Native African Christian Church
Native Congregational Church

APPENDIX III

Native Congress Catholic Church
Native Denomination Church of South Africa
Native Modern Religious Society of East Africa
Native Nation Union Church
National Native Apostolic Church
National Protestant Church in Zion
National Swazi Native Apostolic Church of Africa
National Church of Ethiopia in South Africa
National Baptist Church of South Africa
National Convention Church of New Jerusalem
National African Church of Salom
National Church of God Apostolic in Jerusalem Church
South African Gaza Mission
Seventh Day Baptist Church
Seventh Day Baptist Church of London
Seventh Church of God
St. Philip's Ethiopian Church of South Africa
St. Peter's Apostolic Church
Spade Reen Gemeentes van Zuid Africa
Star Baptist Church
Tembu Catholic Church of South Africa
Transvaal Basuto Church
Transvaal Basuto Lutheran Church
The Supreme Apostolic Church of South Africa
The True (Truth) Zion Church of God
United African Apostolic Church
United Bantu Lutheran Church
United Free Independent Church
United Ethiopian Catholic Church of Africa
United National Catholic Church of Zion
United National Congress Church
United National Church in Africa

THE SEETHING AFRICAN POT

United Church of the Brethren in Zion
United African Missionary Society
United Churches of Christ
United Independent National Church of God
Universal Church of Christ
Union Apostolic Church of South Africa
Uhlanga, or Church of the race
Ukuranye Mission
Universal National Christian Union
Unto the Church of God Apostolic Jerusalem in Zion
Volks Kerk van Zuid Africa
Vula Zingene Yehova e-Zion
Watchtower movement
Zion Brethren Mission Apostolic Church in South Africa
Zion Gospel African Church
Zion Revelation Apostle Church of South Africa
Zion Apostolic Faith Mission
Zion Apostolic Gaza Church of South Africa
Zion Apostolic in Jerusalem Church
Zion Apostolic New Jerusalem in South Africa Church
Zion Christian Church
Zion Mission African Apostolic Church
Zion City Apostolic Paulus Church in South Africa
Zion Holy Church Nation of South Africa
Zulu Congregational Church
Zulu or African Ethiopian Church
Zulu Ethiopian Church